The Songs
of the
People of God

CHARLES HAURET

The Songs
of the
People of God

Translated by
John F. McDonnell, O.P.

THE PRIORY PRESS, CHICAGO, ILL.

Revisores Ordinis: Augustine Rock, O.P.; Bernard O'Riley, O.P. *Imprimi potest*: Gilbert J. Graham, O.P., Provincial. *Nihil obstat*: Bernard O'Riley, O.P., Censor Deputatus. *Imprimatur*: ✠ Most Rev. Cletus F. O'Donnell, J.C.D., Administrator, Archdiocese of Chicago, August 16, 1965.

Library of Congress Catalogue Number 65-19360
© Copyright 1965 by The Priory Press
2005 South Ashland Avenue, Chicago, Illinois 60608
Manufactured in the United States of America

Table of Contents

PART 1
General Notions

PART 2
The Psalms in Their Literary Types

Foreword

This book is addressed to all those who love the Psalms, and especially to those privileged ones who take up the noble and fruitful, but demanding, task of officially perpetuating the sacrifice of praise in the Church. It offers them neither a new translation, a detailed explanation, nor a spiritual paraphrase. It does not keep them from having recourse to standard introductions and commentaries, but it will help them to enter the intimacy of the psalmists. It will help them to appreciate the work of those inspired men—men of prayer and poets—and especially help to carry on the canticles of Israel in Christian song and to express the prayer of today in the accents of an older time.

PART 1

General Notions

[1]
Obstacles

A problem carefully outlined is more easily resolved. A question well stated spurs research and may even suggest the right answer. Some sick people feel themselves almost at the point of recovery when they discover deep in their subconscious the secret reasons of their illness. The clear exposure of obstacles prepares us to surmount them. The Psalter arouses enthusiasm and difficulty by turns. It always attracts and often charms but it is sometimes disappointing. St. Augustine wrote: "My Psalter, my joy!" When we recite the Psalms, intricately woven into the fabric of the Divine Office, we encounter so many obstacles, that in spite of our good will we suffer at times from a seeming lack of harmony between our soul and the psalmody. We must be careful neither to ignore the five causes of this painful disagreement nor to minimize them. Rather, let us at the beginning take inventory of the difficulties, though met in differing degrees, of praying the Psalms. This preliminary inquiry, moreover, will give us the opportunity to place the problems of the Psalter in proper perspective.

11

THE PSALMS: OUTDATED

Even in our contemporary world, the gap from one generation to another is often broad enough to cause misunderstanding and a lack of comprehension. Such discord is even more understandable when caused by the separation of a number of centuries. It is almost impossible to share mind and heart with a people who lived so long before us and who were part of a society quite different from our own.

The greater number of Psalms, according to the most widespread opinion, date back before the Babylonian exile (the sixth century B.C.), some of them to the time of David (tenth century B.C.), and some even before the institution of the kingship (eleventh century B.C.). Ordinarily, among the most venerable mentioned,[1] are the hymns in honor of the Ark of the Covenant (23:7-10; 46). These poems are sung either by the king[2] or on his behalf. A searching glance at other scattered pieces contains allusions to events of great antiquity.[3]

To be sure, archaism is of passionate interest to scholars who are lovers of any work overlaid with the patina of the centuries. A bit of pedantic snobbery,

---

[1]The Psalms are always cited according to the numbering of the Vulgate used in the liturgical books. It is generally one number lower than that of the Hebrew text. Biblical references that name no book are to be found in the Psalter. The translation is generally that of the Confraternity version. Where the commentary demands, the translator has made his own version. These cases are noted.

[2]Pss. 2, 17, 19, 20, 44, 60, 62, 71, 109.

[3]Pss. 45, 47, 59, 75, 79.

however, at times slips into the fervor of certain contemporary opinions about antiquity. But for those who
prefer to reach out to the future rather than to dwell
on the past, the antiquity of a prayer is not a particularly good recommendation. On the other hand, some
exegetes would lessen the distance separating us from
the psalmists. To be sure, the names of Moses (89:1),
of David (73 times), and of Solomon (71:1; 126:1)
figure in the headings of the Psalms, but these references do not carry sufficient conviction. These headings,
added in the course of the centuries, represent memories
worthy of respect, but they are the relics of traditional
commentaries and not necessarily objective information
about the origin of these works.

In reality, psalmody flourished in the liturgy of the
second Temple, after the return from the Exile (538
B.C.). The Davidic halo[4] given many of the poems by
the Fathers has vanished, but David is nonetheless
considered the originator of sacred poetry—its most notable author, its verifier, and the spiritual father of the
inspired poets because he embodies perfectly the qualities of the just man persecuted, the reconciled penitent,
and the figure of the Messiah.

The definitive redaction of the Psalms should then
be placed after the Babylonian captivity. If we correct
this position by an important distinction, we shall probably get close to true liturgical poetry. Although relatively late in time, it nonetheless comes down from

[4]In particular, Pss. 2, 15, 17, 31, 50, 68, 109.

age-old traditions. Later composers brought the works of their predecessor back by taking over and adopting ancient material. At times, they placed archaic fragments of the royal, Davidic, premonarchic and, perhaps, even relics of religious literature of neighboring peoples from Mesopotamia, Phoenicia, and Egypt[5] in a new setting.

The entangled and difficult question of the chronology of the Psalms and the weight to be given foreign influences will long be a matter of discussion. In any case, the Psalms are related to us as not only old, but very old—so old as even to be out-of-date. As prayer, they indeed seem out of date, for who would put new wine in old bottles?

FOREIGN TO OUR CULTURE

There is another difficulty. In this poetry, the fruit of Semitic genius, words often take on meanings unknown to our dictionaries. Words such as *truth, justice, salvation, fear, knowledge of God, peace, glory, name, soul,* and *spirit* do not represent the same reality as the corresponding English terms of today. The evocative value of many metaphors is frequently lost, for these figures presuppose obsolete ideas about nature and the universe and social customs long since abolished. The stubborn snake that stops its ears (57:5); the eagle forever young (102:5); the horns of the just and of the wicked (74:5-6, 11); the oil that perfumes the head and runs over on the beard (22:5; 132:2; 140:5); the

[5]Cf. Pss. 18:2-7; 28, 67, 73, 81, 103.

allotted cup (10:6, 15:5); the lamp (131:17) are several examples. These images and many others lose their evocative power either wholly or in part for Western man. Naming different parts of the human body (nose, heart, liver, kidneys, bowels) as expressive of feeling is inspired by oversimplified ideas of human physiology and psychology. Finally, the methods of Hebrew poetry, with its diverse forms of parallelism, rules of prosody, and the technique of the alphabetic Psalms,[6] do not coincide with our canons of poetry. It would seem that to pray the Psalms one must change himself into rabbi, archaeologist, and literary critic simultaneously.

A Changed and Worn Formulary

The ancient poems are often obscure documents. They have undergone serious changes in the course of their transmission through the ages. Some specialists labor at re-establishing their primitive tenor. Although they put science, erudition, and imagination to work, there remains much uncertainty in their ingenious reconstructions. Comparison among the more recent translations evokes only wonder. One can hardly find his way among the manifold versions of the *Dixit Dominus*. A priest can hardly identify the strophes in *Conserva me, Deus*—stanzas which from the time of his entrance into the clerical life have echoed in his memory. At times these divergences can be a temptation to disillusioned skepticism. The enigmas or the obscurities of the text may foster the sense of mystery for some, but

[6]Pss. 9, 24, 33, 36, 110, 111, 118, 144.

it is doubtful whether they are favorable to piety even in these cases.

TEXT WITHOUT CONTEXT

If we knew the circumstances surrounding the composition of each Psalm and its real-life setting, the interpretation would become clearer and, consequently, our attention more easily directed. Unfortunately, we lack this precious information. We do not know what mysterious personages are hidden behind the enemies who surround so many of the psalmists nor what lamentable events are deplored in the collective supplications,[7] whether it is the fall of Jerusalem in 586 B.C., the trials of the Maccabaean period, or some other national catastrophe. Here and there, vague references to the history of Judah or of Israel may be gleaned. But if we try to set these up as landmarks, they disappear like a mirage. They are illusions rather than allusions. Attempts to order the poems of the Psalter in a sequence corresponding to Israel's history end in contradictory and disappointing results. Thirteen Psalms[8] should, according to their titles, concern precise episodes in the life of David, but it would be excessive optimism to claim that the content of these Psalms is in agreement with the stories in the Books of Samuel. An impression slowly but surely works its way into our minds: the Psalms, without any real connection with life, without support in history, are lost in an atmosphere that is both vague and inconsistent.

[7] Pss. 43, 73, 78, 79.
[8] Pss. 3, 7, 17, 33, 50, 51, 53, 55, 56, 58, 59, 62, 141.

INHERITANCE OF AN OUTMODED LITURGY AND PIETY

Some exegetes, aware of the impossibility of arranging the Psalms in time, try instead to connect them with the liturgical cycle of the Temple. They think that placing them within the framework of worship can take the place of a historical setting. This hypothesis, in part plausible, creates a new difficulty. The greater part of Psalms, if not all of them, were born in worship and for worship. Therefore, it would be reasonable to state that the disappearance of a liturgical context would result in nullity of the text itself. If these prayers are fitted for Jewish ritual, how can they be acclimated to a Christian setting? A plant uprooted from the soil that nourishes it risks withering and death.

An essential aspect of the prayer of the Old Testament runs counter to our modern feelings. The individual who prays is submerged in the group, and the person is lost in the collectivity. Even when the psalmist prays in the first person, he is never freed from his community so that the *we* tends constantly to supplant the *I*. Some exegetes, overly impressed by this fact, wrongly advocate a collective interpretation of the greater part of the Psalms. Christian personalism lends itself badly to this sort of piety. In the past, the group was pre-eminent; today the individual ranks first. These two points of view are clearly opposed. While we wish to set forth our own needs, our own preoccupations, and our own business, the biblical way of speech continually brings us back to the community point of view. Modern studies, far from reassuring us, aggravate our embarrassment. The psalmists, we are told, poured their thought into traditional molds and used a conventional framework inherited from a far distant past. How can this hieratic, fossilized terminology be reconciled with a personal piety surging from the heart? How can one sing forth his life and live his song with formulae of this sort? Authentic prayer is not fed on literary cliches.

Grave Deficiencies in Teaching

The main obstacle belongs to the order of religion. Weighty imperfections and well-known omissions disfigure the prayer of the Old Testament in the domains of dogma and moral.

The psalmist's supplications were usually limited to the earthly and temporal horizon. Each Sunday, at Vespers, the *Beatus vir qui timet Dominum* is sung. But the happiness of the just man did not go beyond perspectives of the here below. His happiness and well-being derived from a numerous posterity, strong sons ready to defend their father in dispute at the gates of the city, riches, success in business, an excellent reputation, undisturbed peace, the destruction of enemies, and a long life (1, 111, 127). There was no question of retribution beyond the grave. This limited concept was justified for the Hebrews who, through the greater part of their history, had no picture of happiness in the life beyond the grave. The condition of man after death was a twilight period that did not merit the name of life.[9] In the world below ground,

[9]Pss. 6:6; 29:10; 87:6; 11-13; 113:26-27.

where all the departed descend to be gathered together, darkness, silence, and oblivion ruled. Hallow beings asleep, benumbed, and without strength peopled the vast city of the dead. They were no more than shadows of men in a shadow of existence. Nor was there any reward possible for these vanishing phantoms. That is why divine blessings repaid the pious Jew in the land of the living: "Heaven is the heaven of the Lord, but the earth he has given to the children of men" (113:24).

The Christian cannot be content with such poor, rudimentary views. Nor can he feel at ease in that suffocating atmosphere, since for him true life exists not in this world but in the bosom of God, in the house of the Father. To the Jew, the earth was most dear, but the earth the Christian aspires to is heaven. Some of the psalmists, in spite of the deficiencies of common teaching, raised themselves toward a higher ideal. Such was the pious Levite, for whom supreme happiness consisted of meditating upon the Law and fulfilling the divine will. He loved the Law for itself, preferred it to riches, and found his pleasure in its observance. This pure, disinterested, spiritual joy eclipsed material and earthly favors (118).

Other elect souls, ahead of their time, found unheard of meanings in the traditional phraseology. They sang of intimacy with God and of their hope for an uninterrupted communion with him. Indeed, they may have foretold delights without end when in glory in the presence of their Lord.[10] These first rays were fleet-

[10]Pss. 15:11; 48:16; 72:23-26.

ing, and still lacking in brightness, but they announced
the coming dawn. Nonetheless, taken as a whole, the
Psalter still leaves the Christian citizen of heaven
(Phil. 3:20) unsatisfied, for there must be difficulty
in putting the prayer of those who do not know at the
service of the aspirations of those who do. At high
noon, light is not sought from a candle.

The liturgy of the Mass prescribes the recital at the
Offertory of a fragment of Psalm 25, *Do me justice,
O Lord.* The *Lavabo,* in its original context, belonged
to a protestation of innocence: "I wash my hands in
innocence and I go around your altar, O Lord" (cf.
7:9; 72:13). The very words of this statement evoke
by contrast the Gospel parable in which the Pharisee
parades his self-satisfaction (Lk. 18:9 ff.). Jesus condemns this sort of self-sufficiency; Christian humility
demands comportment of a different kind.

The Sermon on the Mount forbids rendering evil
for evil; rather it prescribes the love of one's enemies
and the pardon of injuries (Mt. 5:38 ff.). The psalmists,
on the contrary, vigorously applied the law of an eye
for an eye and a tooth for a tooth. When cursed, they
cursed. If unjustly persecuted, they called down on the
heads of their enemies the sufferings their adversaries
had prepared for them. The Gospel condemns these
savage reflexes. A copious anthology of curses for revenge
could be made up of cries taken from the Psalter.[11]
But, it runs counter to the universal charity demanded

[11]Pss. 7, 34, 51, 53, 57, 58, 68, 78, 108, 136.

of the Christian to echo these cries of ferocious hatred and curses against enemies or against pagans in general. Finally, there is the opposition between the yoke which is sweet, celebrated in the liturgy of Christ the King, and the domination of the warlike and despotic monarch exalted in certain Messianic Psalms (2, 109).

The law of Christ is contained in a single word—*love*—the relationship of sons with their Father in heaven. To be sure, it would be committing a grave error to reserve this spiritual attitude to the faithful of the New Testament (cf. Dt. 13:4-5). However, and this is an astonishing discovery, the psalmists, although they were deeply penetrated by the love of God for men, rarely employed the explicit formula *to love God*[12] in their intimate dialogues with the Lord. Ordinarily they replaced it with the pregnant expression *to fear God*. Fear and love represent, it is true, twin and inseparable aspects of an authentic piety, but the follower of Jesus instinctively emphasizes love.

Incontestably, psalmists and Christians do not pray on the same wave length.[13]

---

[12]Pss. 17:2; 30:24; 114:1; 144:20.
[13]See E. Bernimont, "De l'inegale valeur des Psaumes," *Nouvelle Revue Theologique*, LXXXV (1962), 843-52.

[2]

Christian Psalms

In spite of difficulties and obscurities, in spite of imperfections and gaps, the prayer of the Jews constitutes the principal element of Christian liturgy. This astounding fact, singular in the history of religions, is explained by a rational choice, by an option that represents the fruit of experience and faith.

THE CHOICE OF THE CHURCH OF THE MARTYRS

In the beginning, the Church seems to have hesitated in adopting the songs of the synagogue as a whole. During the first two centuries, an original religious poetry flourished in the nascent communities.[1] There were new songs to match a new faith. Several rhythmic passages from the apostolic writings—for example, the hymn to Christ (Phil. 2:6-11); the praise of "the mystery of piety";[2] the baptismal songs of the First Epistle of St. Peter (1:3-5); and the doxologies scattered in the Apocalypse—look like pieces drawn or copied from the liturgy. Some fragments of this poetry from the springtime of

---

[1] Cor. 14:26; Col. 3:16; Eph. 5:19-20; Jas. 5:13.
[2] Tm. 3:16; cf. Eph. 1:4-14; Col. 1:15-20.

the Church have come down to us.[3] In primitive Christian worship, the Psalter was also used, but less as a collection of songs than as a book for reading, for it was placed in the framework of the proclamation of the prophecies.[4] Following this—the clearest ancient testimonies date from the year 200 B.C.—the Church of the martyrs chose the old collection of *Tehillim*, "praises" or "lauds," for its everlasting praise (*laus perennis*) in honor of God. This adoption was the equivalent of a profession of faith. The community claimed the entire Bible as its patrimony, declared itself the guardian of all the Scriptures, and, in particular, announced that it was the continuation of the Assembly of prayer formerly constituted by Israel. This was no confiscation of the goods of one by another, but the taking of its own inheritance. To be sure, a special circumstance influenced the Church in incorporating the Psalter into her official prayer. Certain heterodox influences, especially Gnostic ones, were infiltrating the faithful; and these innovators gladly used songs to inject their poison. Marcion spread a Psalter of his own composition. And Bardesanes, a heretic of the second century, published a tendentious edition of the 150 Psalms which was spread far and wide throughout the Syriac church. The Manicheans and Arius success-

[3]Cf. Adalbert Hamman, *Prières des premiers chrétiens* (Paris: André Fayard, 1952).

[4]Cf. B. Fischer, "La dévotion aux Psaumes dans 1 'Eglise des Martyrs," *La Maison Dieu*, XXVII (1951).

fully used the same tactics. Thus, in the first centuries, heterodoxy was spread in song.

The Church set up a dike, the Psalter of Israel, against the invasion. At such a juncture, the deliberate choice of Hebrew prayer was pointedly a reaction. It is, therefore, an error to interpret the permanence of the Psalter in our liturgy as a sign of conservatism and of routine, the simple survival of an ancestral practice.

This faraway history enlightens us as to the constant tradition of the Church, and in particular, to its tenacious resistance to counsel, however urgent, that the well-intentioned faithful have never ceased to lavish on her. From time to time, her children have indeed pressed their mother to retire the Psalter as a collection long outmoded and non-Christian, and to fashion a younger collection of spiritual songs, better adapted to the spirit of the Gospel and more in harmony with the aspirations of today. But *Mater Ecclesia,* without excluding eventual accommodations, persists in drawing from the "waters of Siloe that flow gently"; she refuses to slake her thirst at the "river" which unloosens ruin (Is. 8:6 ff.). She mistrusts oversimplified and hazardous solutions.

Recently, in reforming the Breviary, she lightened the burden of the Office and suppressed many lessons. But she still persists in proposing to her sons and imposing on them the prayer of their fathers in the faith. She consents only to purifying, to remolding the ancient repertory in order to produce a revised and corrected version, a Christian re-edition. Yet, the easy and simple suggestions for wiping out the archaism and particularism of the Jewish poems are many. It would seem simple enough, for example, to replace Israel by the people of God, or the sons of God; to erase Sion and Jerusalem and substitute for them the Church or the community; and to introduce the mention of the races of the earth in place of the tribes of Yahweh. Nothing, it seems, could be simpler and more attractive. Here, as an example, is how Psalm 124 would look with some such light retouching:

> They who trust in the Lord
> Are like a mountain
>   which is immovable;
> Which forever stands
> Like the mountains that surround a city,
> Thus is the Lord round about his people,
> Both now and forever . . .
>   peace be upon the children of God! (1-2,5)

Renovation has undeniable advantages in the short run, but its cost is dear. A well-bred child never fails to recognize his own mother, in spite of the wrinkles that furrow her face. In like manner, the Church cannot dream of forgetting its origins or even pretend to be ignorant of its prophetic prehistory. It has just shown with bold initiative that, far from modernizing the Psalms, she searches rather for their old face.[5] The *old* Psalter is the Psalter of the Church.

[5]"We have ordered the appearance of a new Latin version of the Psalms to follow closely and faithfully the original texts." Pope Pius XII, Motu Proprio, "In cotidianis precibus," *Acta Apostolicae Sedis,* XXXVII (1945), 66.

Historical circumstances influenced the choice made by the Church. While some call the decision of religious authority one of opportunism, others boast of good taste displayed by the heads of the Church. The poetic value of many of the Psalms, in any case, will always strike with wonder souls sensitive to artistic beauty. Some of these poems[6] will always appear in anthologies, but not all of them can claim the rank of master works. To be sure, there are pure flames in the Psalter, but there are cinders as well. The universal and the catholic bearing of many of the songs cannot help but strike every mind.

There were psalmists who would subscribe to the verse of Terence: "I am a man and consider nothing human foreign to me." The Psalter in revealing its authors, pictures them as men above all. Thought should also be given to that magnificent storehouse of spiritual experience hoarded in these venerable prayers, murmured during centuries by one of the most religious people of the world. Some fragments of these songs may have echoed in the old shrines of Palestine, at Dan, Silo, and Bethel: a greater number in the sanctuary of Solomon. But the greatest part of all was used in the second Temple and in the synagogues. The Psalter is reckoned among the most familiar texts of the fervent community of Qumran. "We are born with this book in our bowels," a Jewish author wrote not

[6]Cf. 28, 44, 45, 47, 83, 89, 103.

long ago.[7] However, all these things—opportunism, estheticism, psychology, humanism, historical consideration—taken together still do not fully account for the adoption of the Psalter.

The fundamental reason, to be precise, lies in the unique prerogative of biblical prayer: its inspiration by God. Under the guidance of the Holy Spirit, the Church turned instinctively with a sort of supernatural sympathy toward the prayer breathed forth by the Spirit. She thus entered into the possession of a formulary, sacred in its origin and guaranteed by the privilege of inerrancy. She received it in faith and continues to keep it with reverence, gratitude, and trust. She neither corrects nor remakes it. Nothing will again tear her away from these words which, for her, are sweeter than syrup or honey from the comb (18:11).

We must let our conduct be guided by that of the Church. Nevertheless, historical and doctrinal justification does not clear away all obstacles. The essential difficulty remains: How are we, Christians of the twentieth century, to thrill in harmony with ancient Jewish poets, inspired though they be?

THE PSALMS: PRAYERS OF CHRIST

One indisputable fact throws decisive light on the problem: Jesus prayed the Psalms. From that moment on, none dared to qualify as non-Christian (or as

[7]A. Chouraqui, *Les Psaumes* (Paris: Presses Universitaires de France, 1956), p. 1.

inassimilable by Christians) texts recited by Christ our Lord.

The world honored the Psalter at Nazareth. When the Virgin Mary improvised her *Magnificat,* she spontaneously borrowed both themes and words from the traditional psalmody. In this connection, St. Augustine gave to the Virgin (as a follower of Mariam, sister of Moses and ancestress of the psalmists [cf. Ex. 15:20-21]), the evocative title of she "who leads our chorus."[8] Mary taught her son the hymns of his people. When Jesus reached the age of twelve, "son of the commandment," he joined the crowd of pilgrims on march to Jerusalem singing the songs of ascent (119-133). Each year, on the occasion of great feasts that mark the path of the liturgical cycle—Passover, Pentecost, Tabernacles, and the Dedication of the Temple[9]—he joined in public prayer. More often, at the synagogue of Nazareth (Lk. 4:16), he took part in the psalmody which, by custom, served to frame the readings of the Law and of the Prophets.[10]

The Gospels contain even more precise indications that the Psalms convey the priestly prayer of Christ.

[8]The text is cited in the Sixth Lesson of the Office of the eighth of September. *Sermon on the Annunciation of our Lord; PL* 39:2105.

[9]Jn. 2:13; 5:1; 7:10; 10:22-23: 12:12.

[10]Cf. Robert Aron, *Jesus of Nazareth: The Hidden Years,* trans. Frances Frenaye (New York: William Morrow and Company, 1962). A. Arens has tried to give the Psalms their setting in the liturgy of the synagogue; cf. *Die Psalmen in Gottesdienst des Alten Bundes* (Trier: Paulinus-Verlag, 1961).

The Last Supper closes (Mt. 26:30) with the recital of the *Hallel* (112-117). Thus, after the institution of the Holy Eucharist, Jesus, mediator of the New Covenant and founder of the ultimate form of worship, applies to himself the canticles of the Old Testament. "The cup of salvation I will take up, and I will call upon the name of the Lord . . . . Precious in the eyes of the Lord is the death of his faithful ones . . . . To you I will offer a sacrifice of thanksgiving (115:4-6, 8). I shall not die but live . . . . The stone which the builders rejected has become the cornerstone . . . . This is the day the Lord has made; let us be glad and rejoice in it" (117:17,22,24). The ancient formulae —"cup of salvation," "precious death," "sacrifice of thanksgiving," "life forever," "cornerstone," "day of the Lord in cheerfulness"—when consciously taken up by the Savior, became personal on his lips and tragically laden with a new meaning. They became the expression of an ardent prayer, in spirit and in truth. There is no incompatibility here between a liturgy stigmatized as stereotyped or fossilized, and spontaneous living prayer. Even on his arrival at Gethsemane, Jesus expressed his anguish in words inspired, as it seems, by Psalm 41, the plaint of an exiled Levite: "My soul is sorrowful even unto death."[11] On the cross, the Son turned toward his Father. Nothing could be more intimate, more original, and inexpressible than this movement of one whose very being is defined precisely

[11]Mt. 26:38; Mk. 14:34; cf. Jn. 12:27.

by his relation to his Father. Yet, at that supreme moment, the very summit of his mission, Jesus breathed forth his most profound filial feelings in the words that open Psalm 21: "My God, My God, why hast thou forsaken me?" (Mt. 27:46; Mk. 15:34.) The cry of the just man suffering, but always in communion with God, expresses exactly the distress, the love, and the unshakable trust of Christ crucified (cf. Jn. 19:20-29; Ps. 68:22).

Further, the Savior breathes his last while murmuring a verse of Psalm 30: "Father, into thy hands I commend my spirit" (Lk. 23:46). He substitutes expressly his "I" for the *I* of the psalmist, and absorbs, so to speak, the psalmist's personality as he uses his words. In the course of the Last Supper, he acted in the same way when he fixed his eyes on Judas and declared: "He who eats my bread has lifted his heel against me."[12] With good reason, St. Augustine called Jesus "that wonderful singer of Psalms" (*Christus, inste cantator psalmorum*).

THE PSALMS: PRAYERS ABOUT CHRIST

Jesus was hero as well as singer, and the texts he used were about himself. As a master of exegesis, he introduced his Apostles to the Christian interpretation of Scripture: "All things must be fulfilled that are written in the law of Moses and the Prophets and the Psalms concerning me" (Lk. 24:44). He himself made

[12]Mk. 14:18; Jn. 13:18=Ps. 40:10.

use of this principle in a memorable discussion with
the Pharisees about Psalm 109 (Mt. 22:41-46). The
title of "Lord" given by David to the Messiah and the
transcendence of the king seated at the right hand of
God announced the mystery of his person (cf. Jn.
10:34; Ps. 81:6). He had recourse to the same argument before the Sanhedrin to give a glimpse of his
future glory and of his return at the end of time.[13]
He sprinkled his discourses with quotations or reminiscences from the Psalter.[14] The Apostles and writers
of the New Testament, as faithful disciples practiced
the method taught and illustrated by their master.
They gleaned in the Psalter many "testimonies" in
which their keen-sighted love discovered the figure of
their Savior drawn in advance. His whole career was
sketched, not only in broad outline, but in detail. On
the cross, Jesus had intoned Psalm 21, which opened
the eyes of the disciples so that the sacred authors
sought and found in the prayer of the persecuted innocent many connections with the circumstances of
the Passion.[15] They had no hesitation in lengthening

[13]Mt. 26:64 and parallels; cf. Mt. 21:42=Ps. 117:22-3;
Mt. 23:39; Lk. 13:35=Ps. 117:26.

[14]Mt. 5:4=Ps. 36:11; Mt. 5:35=Ps. 47:3; Mt. 7:23=Ps.
6:9; Mt. 8:11=Ps. 106:3; Mt. 18:12=Ps. 118:176; Mt.
16:27=Ps. 61:13; Lk. 10:19=Ps. 90:13; Lk. 19:44=Ps.
136:9; Lk. 21:25=Ps. 64:8-9.

[15]Mt; 27:39=Ps. 21:8; Mt. 27:43=Ps. 21:9; Jn. 19:24=
Ps. 21:19.

the list of citations for their allusions.[16] Yet, it is a remarkable coincidence that the cited texts were borrowed most often from individual supplications. Jesus applied to himself (or the sacred writers applied to him) the lamentations of the sick, of the persecuted, of the accused, and of the poor—for the Savior is laden with the wretchedness of all (Mt. 8:17). He summed up in his own person the distress of all. He applied to himself the prayer of mankind at grips with sorrow. He is the just man suffering, the man persecuted without cause. He is the innocent accused, the exile, the meek, and the poor. The Savior incorporated diverse situations and relived them in his own fashion, that is to say, as the Son of God. The argument of Jesus with the Pharisees on the subject of Psalm 109 opened the way for the Messianic exegesis of the royal poems (2, 44, 88, 109). For the true son of David was also Jesus. Thus, thanks to this shadowy and diffused "Messianism," the Psalter breathes forth Christ. Jesus fulfilled the Law and the Prophets. He also brought to their conclusion the predictions, the shadowy sketches, and the presentiments of Old Testament prayer. He perfected the supplications, the praises, and thanksgivings of Israel and gave them full meaning, ultimate consecration, and sovereign efficacy. He did not lessen their

[16]Ps. 21:23, cf. Heb. 2:12; Ps. 26:12; 34:11, cf. Mk. 14:55-7; Ps. 34:18, cf. Mt. 27:39; Ps. 39:7-9, cf. Heb. 10:5-10; Ps. 68:5, cf. Jn. 15:25; Ps. 68:10, cf. Jn. 2:17 and Rom. 15:3; Ps. 68:22, cf. Mt. 27:34; Ps. 77:2, cf. Mt. 13:35; Ps. 117:22, cf. Mk. 12:10 and Rom. 9:33; Ps. 17:50, cf. Rom. 15:9.

integrity but consecrated it—*Integritate non minuit sed sacravit.*[17] At last we can grasp in depth the reasons why the Church has received, preserved, and defended these inspired prayers. It is because the Spouse discerns in the Psalms, by love's infallible intuition, the face of her Lord.

THE PSALMS: PRAYERS TO CHRIST

At a very early date, the community transferred to Christ the passages that the Psalter addressed to God. When Pliny pointed out to Trajan that the Christians assembled on a fixed day before the rising of the sun to chant alternately a hymn to Christ as (to) God (*tanquam Deo*), he was alluding in all probability to the liturgical psalmody. The first Christians, according to weighty evidence, prayed to their Lord—*Kyrios*—using the Psalms.[18] Jesus came with finesse and discretion, pointing out the path to his disciples. On Palm Sunday, the priest and the scribes were enraged at the children's shouts in honor of Jesus. The Lord accepted the homage of the little ones and, to the confusion of the wise, he called their attention to Psalm 8: "Out of the mouths of babes and sucklings thou hast perfected praise" (Mt. 21:16). There was no difference between the praise of God and that of Christ. We have only to open a missal to note that the Church, on the

[17]Cf. A. George, "Jesus et les Psaumes" in *À la rencontre de Dieu. Mémorial Gelin* (Bibliothèque de la Faculté de Théologie de Lyon, Vol. 8; Le Puy: Éditions Xavier Mappus, 1961), pp. 297-308.

[18]Heb. 1:10-12; Eph. 4:8; 1 Pt. 2:3; Heb. 1:6.

feasts of the Lord, invites us to pray to Jesus in terms used by the psalmists in their dialogue with God.

CHRIST, FOCAL CENTER OF THE PSALMS

The intention of God, principal author of the Psalms, is discussed here. Two theological principles explain the fashion in which Jesus, as well as the writers of the New Testament, and the Church acted.

First of all, there is the dogma of biblical inspiration. The Psalms and every other part of the Bible have God as their author, but he foresees all and sets all in order. He can, if he will, foretell by the psalmist in express and direct terms the person and the work of the Savior. Indeed, the intention of God, the inspirer of the sacred books, falls primarily and above all on his Anointed One. Likewise, the history of the world had its focus on the coming of the Incarnate Word. Thus, the separate sections of the Bible converged upon Jesus. In virtue of this principle, the Fathers and the ancient commentators chose to multiply prophetic prayers exclusively about the Messiah. They read in the Psalter, as in a sort of tracery, the anticipation of the Gospel.[19]

Modern exegetes, while more reserved, still do not depart essentially from this tradition. Rather, they agree on a preponderant importance of the *sensus plenior* (plenary sense) of the Psalms which broadens, deepens, and prolongs in a homogeneous and organic fashion the obvious intent of the text. In the same manner, a

[19]Cf. P. Salmon, *Les "Tituli Psalmorum" des manuscrits latins* (Paris: Éditions du Cerf, 1961).

seed opens and spreads itself. God inspired in the psalmists opinions which contained a determined and sufficient meaning for them—the first literal sense. Besides this, the principal author, by his sovereign thought and will, joined to the text a plus value that would be verified in the mystery of Christ and of his Church—the second literal sense or the plenary sense. This added meaning was not usually evident in the consciousness of the poets and is veiled from the investigation of philologists and critics as well. But it is unveiled by Jesus and the sacred writers, quickened by the same Spirit who guided the psalmists. Thanks to his authentic interpreters, the principal author reveals his whole thought, uncovers his final intent, and delivers the secret of his intentions. God himself again takes up, makes precise, and curiously comments on his own word.[20] Let us therefore not qualify as pure coincidence, as fortuitous meetings, or, as ingenious, these connections made by Jesus or the writers of the New Testament. Jesus, by citing many passages of the Psalms, made it abundantly clear that the Holy Spirit thought of him when inspiring the Psalms.

[20]Cf. Pierre Benoit, "La plénitude de sens des Livres Saints," *Revue Biblique*, LXVII (1960), 161-96. "The priest or sister who recites the Psalms cannot apply them to Christ, to the Church, or to his own soul without continually using the fuller sense" (p. 193).

MASTER OF HISTORY

Our second truth is the agreement of the two Testaments.[21] Between the Jewish and Christian economies there exists in God's plan, not a simple succession, but a continuity whereby the old is surpassed by the new. God, as master of history, prepared the world for the Incarnation of his Son. The first Covenant, provisory and imperfect, consists of a promise, an expectation, and a foreshadowing of the second perfect and final Covenant. The Old Testament is a mere shadow of the future reality. It is Christianity, but in silhouette. So, too, are the analogies and mysterious correspondence between the two phases of sacred history (people, events, personages, institutions, liturgy, prayer). This intimate connection, resulting from a divine intention, makes lawful the principle of Christian interpretation of the Psalter, without at the same time justifying every application made by commentators. It authorizes us, in particular, to look for the typical sense.

In this case, appeal is made to "the meaning that God has given to the realities of the new economy of which they were the preparation and the prediction, a signification which normally escaped the authors who

[21]Joseph Coppens, *Les harmonies des deux Testaments. Essai sur les divers sens de l'Écriture et sur l'unité de la Révélation* (Paris: Casterman, 1949); P. Grelot, *Sens chrétien de l'Ancien Testament* (Paris-Tournai:Desclée et Cie, 1962); C. Larcher, *L'actualité chrétienne de l'Ancien Testament* (Paris: Éditions du Cerf, 1962). The Protestant theologian treats the same subject in his work *L'Ancien Testament dans l'Église* (Neuchâtel-Paris; Delachaux et Niestlé, 1960).

narrated them but which God knew and which he sowed in the sacred text in advance as a seed of future revelation" (P. Benoit). The Christian does not invent this second meaning but discovers it. The risk is run of falsifying the perspectives of the history of salvation if, by an excessive care for immediate efficacy, one strikes from the Psalter those pretended archaisms which are in reality, for better trained eyes (that is to say Christian ones), the anticipations, the landmarks, and the points of attachment. The two Testaments are linked together and, what is more important, penetrate one another. The fundamental tone of the Psalter is Jewish, but the harmonics are Christian.

CONCLUSION

Psychology completes the data of theology. It teaches us that words are only a relative means of expression with a rather elastic value. Each one treats them in the measure of his own interior riches. This law is verified especially in formulae of prayer. A full soul restates and relives the text, giving it a new content. An empty soul is limited to repeating it like an automaton. At times the psalmists used the same vocabulary and the same themes as the religious poets of Phoenicia, Babylonia, or Egypt. In some cases, the hypothesis that this represents borrowing may be defended. But the fact of the matter gives the Book of Psalms an unexpected range. By handing down to us fossils from the inheritance of the pagan nations, the Psalter becomes the archive of universal piety. It binds us again, over the centuries, to men of long ago in quest of an unknown god, who, led astray by paganism, only babbled their prayers. The psalmists often spoke in the same words, but their expression, integrated into an absolutely different intellectual and spiritual synthesis, took on an original accent.

With them, there was no longer polytheism but an intransigent monotheism, no longer magic, but the Covenant. Righteousness succeeded depravity. Instead of mythological exploits there were the great deeds of God in nature and history. As the Jewish community progressed in light and revelation through success and in spite of setbacks, generations of believers within it recited the same praises and the same supplications. But, at different levels and at different stages of tradition on the march, the Psalms reflect a more or less refined piety, a more or less rich spirituality. They lend themselves so much more easily to being read anew, to being reinterpreted, because they abound in broad and imprecise formulae. Divorced from time, they are universal and impersonal. The malleability of the vocabulary permits varied applications and manifold adaptations to concrete life,[22] individually or nationally. Finally, in the fullness of time, a child of Israel, the

[22]Albert Gelin "Comment le peuple d'Israel lisait l'Ancien Testament" in *L'Ancien Testament et les Chrétiens* (Paris: Éditions du Cerf, 1951), pp. 117 ff.; "La question des 'reletcures' bibliques a l'interieur d'une tradition vivante" in J. Coppens, A. Descamps, and É. Massaux, editors, *Sacra Pagina* (Gembloux: Éditions J. Duculot, 1959), I, pp. 303-13; Henri Cazelles, "Une relecture du Psaume XXIX" in *Mémorial Gelin*, pp. 119-28.

ineffable One, the Son of God, Savior of men, and leader of the multitude of the redeemed in his turn, takes up the ancient prayers to express his own unique experience. He says them anew, not just over again, because he lives them anew. He raises them and makes them right and adds to them. He inaugurates, for the use of his followers, a new style of prayer.[23] Christians, the spiritual posterity of Abraham, will from this time forward sing to the Lord a new song (149:1). There is no need to change the texts, but to weight them with their own feelings as adopted sons of God, brothers of Christ, joined with him in the redemption of the world. They have learned the secret of changing obstacles into launching platforms.

[23]Cf. C. Larcher, *op. cit.*, pp. 45 ff.

[3]

Our Prayer

The preceding reflections clearly indicate how prayer must be oriented. They also suggest to us the means of victory over the obstacles which the devil's advocate has been so kind as to enumerate and even exaggerate. Four words sum up what our personal attitude toward the Psalms should be: *assimilation, advancement, substitution,* and *updating.*

ASSIMILATION

It is indeed a fault of method to linger over abstruse passages. By fixing one's attention on obscure points one forgets to see areas of light. Some minds are weighted down with a fascination for, even an obsession with, obscurity. Yet, stars do illuminate the night. Certain notions, representations, and images in the Psalter seem foreign or only slightly familiar to our modern minds. But we are frankly obliged to recognize, first of all, the indisputable presence of assimilable matter. Rich, abundant, solid, and nourishing substance does exist here. As a matter of fact, the Psalter contains, under the old formulae, permanent, universal, and timeless values that are linked to no country. It is our first task to make ourselves fully willing to appreciate them.

THE HYMNS: RELIGIOUS MEANING OF NATURE

One class of Psalms, the hymns, exalts the perfections of the Creator in all his greatness, omnipotence, goodness, and wisdom. Each one of these songs breaks forth with a "Glory to God in the highest," full of adoration and religious wonder at the works of God. The psalmists never celebrate the beauty and harmony of the universe for their own sakes, but always in praise of the Creator. The *Te Deum* of Psalm 148 orchestrates in lyric fashion the tale of the world's beginning (Gn. 1). The heavens and the sun announce the glory of God (18:2-7). The seven claps of thunder in Psalm 28 display the Lord's unconquerable power in the storm. Then man, the image and vicar of God, is lost in wonder at the sight of the starry sky. He is astonished at the condescension of the Creator in his regard (8:2).[1] All of nature is transformed into a sacrament, visual evidence of God's presence and majesty.[2] These themes do not ever become obsolete. Even in an era of cosmonauts and lunar explorations, they contain an astounding relevance to our time. These scientific exploits with engineering successes could conceivably dull our religious feeling for the universe.

[1] Cf. 103, and the following fragments: 32:6-9; 73:12-17; 88:3-15; 135:5-9.

[2] Cf. Evode Beaucamp, *The Bible and the Universe; Israel and the theology of history,* trans. David Balhatchet (Westminster, Maryland: Newman Press, 1963).

But the hymns, recited without haste, with attention and devotion, neutralize this danger, safeguard our spiritual balance, and compel us to contemplate the cosmos in all of its truth. These songs introduce into our daily lives a truly disinterested prayer. If the Psalter were to disappear from existence, it is doubtful that praise in its purest form would continue to hold a sufficient place in our piety. What is more, the spiritual marrow of the hymns is offered to us in an easily-digested form. The psalmists, even when they mention scientific phenomena, make no pretense of scholarship. Neither do they indulge themselves in speculation. There is no science, nor metaphysics, not even abstraction, but a substance adaptable immediately and by everyone.

HISTORY AS DIALOGUE: THE EVIDENCE OF GOD

These remarks are also valid for the Psalms, which recall God's interventions in the past.[3]

History is not a haphazard juxtaposition of events, but a sequence of meetings with God, revealing the Lord as nature does—his power, his wonders, his judgments,[4] and his mercies (102). By his lofty deeds, true theophanies, the Master weaves the web of history.[5] He makes his anger known, proves his faithfulness, shows his grace, and so enters into dialogue with his people. Often these two themes of creation and history are interwoven. Both illustrate the absolute lordship of God. We will find less difficulty in assuming these

[3]Pss. 77, 104, 105; 113:1-8; 135.
[4]Pss. 43, 59, 73, 78, 79, 82, 88.
[5]Pss. 32, 135, 145, 146-147.

historical themes in our prayer if we remember the unity of the plan of salvation and the agreement between the two Covenants. In reality and in the light of faith, all the reverses and glories, setbacks, amendments, and hopes of the Chosen People interest us as family affairs. The adventure of Israel blends into our own spiritual heredity. By the events of another day, God speaks to us and beckons to us in the present. His voice re-echoes in our ears today (94:6-11). The flight of centuries ceases to be an obstacle. We become familiar with great personages, some of whom appear again in the New Testament and in the liturgy: Abraham,[6] Isaac (104:9), Melchisedec (109:4), Moses and Aaron,[7] Samuel (98:6) and David.[8] More obscure personalities such as Dathan, Abiram, and Phinees (105:17, 30), may awake recollections sleeping in our memories. If we remain unreceptive to other names, such as those of Sehon, king of the Amorrites, Og, king of Basan (134:11; 135:19-20), Sisara, Jabin, Oreb, Zeb, Zebee, Salmana (82:10, 12), the serenity of our prayer will not be disturbed. Sites in Palestine or Canaan—such as Lebanon,[9] Hermon,[10] Sichem, and Socchoth (59:8; 107:8); Tabor (88:13); Silo (77:60); Endor (82:11); Ephrata and the field of Jaar (131:6)—pass before our eyes without our feeling that we are away from home.

[6]Pss. 46:10; 104:6, 9, 42.
[7]Pss. 76:21; 98:6; 102:7; 104:26; 105:16, 23, 32.
[8]Pss. 77:70; 88:4, 21, 36, 50; 131:1, 10, 11, 17; 143:10.
[9]Pss. 28:5-6; 36:35; 91:13; 103:16.
[10]Pss. 41:7; 88:13; 132:3.

The Psalms often mention well-known countries and peoples: Egypt,[11] Ethiopia (67:32; 86:4); Assur (82:9); and Babylon (86:4; 136:1, 8); Tyre (44:12; 82:8; 86:4); Gebal or Byblos (82:8); Philistia (82:8; 86:4); Edom,[12] Moab,[13] Amon, Amalec (82:8), and Basan.[14] Uncertainties about the whereabouts of some places named—Salmon (67:15); Ophir (44:10); Tharsis (47: 8; 71:10); and Saba (71:10,15)—do not make the text unintelligible.

The broad lines of God's action are precisely drawn in the Psalter: the epic of the Patriarchs; the going forth from Egypt from the "fields of Tanis" (77:12, 43); the crossing of the Sea of Reeds (105:7,9,22; 135:13); the meeting at Sinai (67:9,18); the faithfulness of God in spite of the thanklessness of men at Horeb (105:19); also at Massa (94:8); at Meriba (80:8; 94:8; 105:32); and at Beelphegor (105:28); the conquest of the Promised Land, the choice of Jerusalem, and finally the election of the dynasty of David, keeper of the Messianic promise (88:20 ff.; 131).

To be sure, some passages still remain shrouded in deep clouds, but a plausible sense filters through generally. The recent Latin translation cannot be reproached for a lack of clarity. Our ignorance of the circumstances

[11]Pss. 67:32; 77:51; 79:9; 80:6, 11; 104:23, 38; 113: 1; 134:8-9; 135:10.
[12]Pss. 59:10; 107:10-11; 136:7.
[13]Pss. 59:10; 82:7; 107:10.
[14]Pss. 21:13; 67:16, 23; 134:11.

surrounding the composition of the Psalms, their date, and their authors in no way compromises the prayer itself. The interest and the value of the canticles dwells in their poetic quality and, above all, in their spiritual meaning. The essential must be separated from the accessory. The precise occasion of certain victory songs (23, 46, 149) escapes us, but this uncertainty by no means prevents us from addressing our praises to the *King of glory, who reigns over peoples and adorns the lowly with victory.*

INDIVIDUAL LAMENTS: EXPRESSIONS OF MANKIND'S LASTING WRETCHEDNESS

The large but compact group of individual lamentations forms the backbone of the Psalter. Yet, these prayers belong to unhappy people of every time and place, and are illustrated by a variety of concrete situations. They emanate from the cruel experiences of life—from the moaning of the sick, the complaint of exiles, and pleas for help by men accused, persecuted, or imprisoned. They tell of the remorse and repentance of sinners, the anguish of minds troubled by life's shortness. They are concerned with the problem of evil and the riddles of the world's governments. In spite of some smudges—the trace of God's instrument—these complaints on the whole express sincerely, and simply, and sometimes in accents of an enviable literary richness, our permanent miseries (physical, moral, spiritual); indeed, the whole gamut of human emotion. The profoundly human character of these pleas for help keeps them ever alive.

Practical Consequences: The Literal Sense and Literary Forms

It is impossible to absorb the substance of the Psalms without, at least, a minimum understanding of the text. Otherwise, one has only a veneer of prayer, artificial and ancient. Normally, it is impossible to grasp the literal sense without serious study, renewed again and again and never really ended. In this matter, apprenticeship is life-long. Thanks to persevering effort, what obscure details there are will gradually be cleared up. Peculiarities of vocabulary, Semitisms, unaccustomed figures of speech, allusions to history, or to customs and ways of life, reminiscences from, or the debris of, extrabiblical literatures, and theological difficulties all will disappear. We pray as we work—by the sweat of our brows.

A summary of indispensable equipment would require a recent introduction to the Psalter, a faithful and poetic English translation, and a commentary, modern but still prudent, traditional yet discerning.

Contemporary exegetes consecrate their efforts to discovering and classifying the literary and spiritual families of the Psalms, also re-creating their original atmosphere. They generally separate these forms: hymns, individual or collective laments, prayers of trust, private or public thanksgiving, royal songs, Psalms of wisdom, liturgies, etc. This classification offers not only a theoretical advantage of the literary or scientific order, but also brings with it a practical advantage. That is, when it is used with discernment and flexibility. Each type of Psalm is characterized by a fairly precise structure.

Those of the same family begin, develop, and conclude in a regular pattern. The hymn and the thanksgiving, for example, do not begin in the same way as the lamentation. The first verses put us on guard, for they already have something to tell us of the form, tonality, and major themes. Thus, at the very start, we are in tune with the psalmist so that contact is immediately established. Literary analysis supports prayer without causing distraction. Its contribution is real if modest, for alone it does not plunge us into the heart of a Psalm, anymore than the knowledge of the human skeleton reveals to us the inner man as he really is. Besides the bones, there are flesh and muscles. Above all, there is life and soul, both inaccessible to the scalpel.[15] The Psalms are, to be sure, literary documents, poetry, but they are above all, prayers, the very breath of believing souls in dialogue with God. It is impossible to understand them without a mysterious sympathy created by sharing a like faith.

ADVANCEMENT

The initial attitude of sympathetic reception and assimilation safeguards us against the fantasies of subjectivism, arbitrary interpretation, and pseudomysticism. From this first stage on, we draw on an authentic "source of spirituality," for the humble literal sense comes from the Spirit. But the example of Jesus, who in his prayer raised the Psalms to his own level, invites

[15]Albert Gelin, *L'âme d'Israél dans le Livre* (Paris: André Fayard, 1958), pp. 46 ff.

us to advance beyond this step. Here are some applications.

THE ROYAL POEMS: CHRIST THE KING

The royal poems, of which there are about ten, celebrate the enthronement of the king (2, 71, 109); his wedding (44); his going forth to war (19); and his victories (17, 20). Some exegetes, faithful to the tradition of the Fathers, treat this or that poem as pure prophecy, foretelling the King of the last days. In reality, these complex Psalms, whose meaning is full of light and shade, had in mind a prince contemporary with the poet. Yet, they treat no isolated personage, but a member of a line or a house, a link in a dynasty, forwarding the divine promise. In these Psalms, the function absorbs the person. This is why the psalmist passes back and forth without transition from the Messiah enthroned on Sion to the Messiah-David, then to the ideal Messiah, according to God's own heart. After the kingdom's fall, Jews still prayed these Psalms; but then their eyes were turned toward the king of the future who would at last make real a program of piety, justice, and peace. As Christians, we turn our eyes toward Christ the King, the purest legacy of David (Lk. 1:32-33). We do not read an adventitious meaning into them; instead we draw a special message from complex content and center our attention on it. The advance beyond is consistent with recognizing God's own son as this descendant of David, according to the flesh. The psalmists, in spite of their intuition and foresight, had no suspicion of that extraordinary goal that the Davidic dynasty would reach. The Christian point of view, then, implies rectification, broadening, and sublimation of the royal poems.

We acclaim Jesus, Son of the Most High (2:7), God (44:7), the only Priest (109:4), universal King and Judge of nations (2:109). We transform the military nationalists and earthly panoply, the vestiges of an age of shadows and symbols, to give them a spiritual meaning. Without denying historical interpretation, we insist on the fuller sense of the text, not its typological bearing alone. The Psalms of the kingdom of God (92; 95-98) hail the coming of the Lord, who inaugurates a universal kingdom of justice and of peace. *The Lord is king.* Many Jews hoped for a temporal, material, and national domination. Jesus, at the very beginning of his ministry, proclaimed the imminence of his rule: "Behold the kingdom of God is at hand" (Mk. 1:15). In his preaching, he set forth in detail its origin, aspects, phases, and demands. We sing the same Psalms as the Jews. But though the formulae are unchanged, the Psalms now celebrate the unheard-of transformation that Christ has worked in the world, and lyrically comment on the "thy kingdom come" of the Our Father. They call for the establishment of an "eternal and universal kingdom, a kingdom of truth and of life, a kingdom of holiness and of grace, a kingdom of justice, of love and of peace." Beyond this, we leave the earthly horizon behind to join the triumphant Church and heaven.

To be sure, we repeat along with the psalmist of old that our King grants his favors to those who yield to his authority. This is still true. We, poor and needy subjects, must still implore God's help in the harsh battle of life just as the Jews did.

But, unlike Israel, we expand our prayer beyond limits to the measure of the unsearchable riches of Christ (Eph. 3:8). The mystery of the Church transforms everything. In spite of all prophecies and preparations, when the Mystical Body of Christ, the true kingdom of God, entered this world, it came suddenly as an absolutely new reality. Here there are continuity and interruption, both evolution and revolution. The chrysalis burst from its cocoon. The seeds, as they ripen, are stripped of their coverings. In our eyes, these strippings play the role of witnesses to an incomplete stage that is surpassed today. The Christian does not consider himself as an evolved Jew, but as a new creature (Gal. 6:15). That is why he is supported by the past and still escapes its limitations. Although linked to the past, he nonetheless stands apart.

The directive of outstripping the past extends to other types of Psalms. For example, it includes those that enumerate the demands of the Covenant (49; 80), of worship (14; 23:3-6), of the Law,[16] and of the canticles in honor of Jerusalem and the temple.[17] Finally, by virture of the same principle, we must sublimate certain religious notions frequently found in individual

[16]Pss. 100; 118; cf. 16:4-5; 17:22-24; 18:8-14; 25:3 ff.
[17]Pss. 47, 83, 86, 121, 132, 136.

supplications. Christ has renewed all things—peace, salvation, redemption, grace, pardon, justice, the Covenant, blessing, inheritance, glory, and the land of the living. The house of God and the assembly of the saints evoke supernatural realities for us, not natural ones. The *Gloria Patria* has, since the fourteenth century, punctuated the recital of the Psalter. It calls us discreetly but repeatedly to raise ourselves to the level of Christian revelation—and stay there.

SUBSTITUTION

The Other Side: House of the Father. We are asked to prolong, to go beyond, and also to substitute. This third directive is especially necessary for understanding the concepts of suffering, enemies, and the world beyond.

The Christian replaces gloomy Sheol, that mournful netherworld, the *infernum* of the Latin translations, with the radiant happiness found in the House of his Father (Jn. 14:2). By doing this, he does not yield to the temptation of underestimating the gift of the present time. The psalmists never failed to recall this gift of God. The appreciation of spiritual gifts does not imply the denial of material realities, for heaven does not lessen the earth's value. But faith in a life beyond establishes an exact hierarchy of values. Where the Christian is sick, afflicted, or persecuted, and prays for healing, deliverance from his distress, protection against his enemies (even a rich existence in freedom and peace), he tempers the tone of his requests. He adds shading to their themes. It is only with his lips that he pronounces words about Sheol. He seeks first of all the kingdom of God with its justice, persuaded that everything else will be added thereunto (Mt. 6:33).

When interpreted in the light of the Gospel, impassioned appeals to divine justice are no longer shocking, or are at least less shocking, on Christian lips. The *Introit* of the Mass of the Martyrs repeats these cries for vengeance: "Let the prisoners' sighing come before you, O Lord; repay our neighbors sevenfold into their bosoms, avenge the blood of your saints which has been shed" (78:11-12). But the spirit of the Gospel substitutes hatred of the sin for hatred of the sinner. These texts, and others like them, drive from our souls a flabby aversion from evil, the cause of so many failures open or masked. Instead, they declare a war without end against sin. The Fathers evaded the difficulty by placing these Psalms on the lips of Christ, the supreme Judge. At first sight, these curses shock us. They conceal, nonetheless, assimilable values—for example, a heroic faith in the justice of God and an unfailing trust in final salvation. The psalmists, "members of God's own household," manifest in their violent complaints against enemies a lack of ceremony that denotes, in short, the familiarity of a son toward a loving and beloved father who is also just and powerful. Yet, they hide these feelings under a rough, hard shell. We must remember, however, that this epoch was a time when the mysteries of God's infinite mercy, his universal plan of salvation, and the last things were still obscure. Those people, when they suffered, gladly identified their cause with that of God, their partner in the Covenant. They employed certain literary clichés, the legacy of a brutal past, for they were little accustomed to abstract distinctions. They did not know how to curse evil without cursing the evil man.[18]

Detesting the Sin without Hating the Sinner. We rightly borrow from the psalmists their cries of sorrow, for we live as they did, in a world strewn with sorrow, marked by illness, persecution, and injustice of every sort. Suffering and death gnaw away at everything, but since Christ has borne our miseries, carried the cross, and offered in sacrifice the sufferings of mankind, we can no longer approach the problem of suffering as the psalmist did. For suffering joins the members to the redemption of Christ and it precipitates everlasting life (Col. 1:24; 2 Cor. 4:17-18).

Blessed Are They Who Suffer! There is a last effort, that of updating and transforming prayer of long ago into the prayer of today. The prayer of the synagogue is changed into the prayer of the Church, and the prayer of the psalmist into a personal prayer.

UPDATING

Prayer of the Church. Those who are devoted by their station in life to the recitation of the Divine Office become "the mouthpiece of the Church" or, in

[18]Cf. E. Charpentier, "Comment prier les 'psaumes de malédiction'?" *Bible et Vie chrétienne,* XLI (1961), 52-57.

a phrase of St. Augustine, "the voice of the whole Christ, head and body." Consequently, every class of Psalm takes on a new dimension by their interpretation. There is the community's praise in the hymns. Laments of the Church Suffering are found individually or collectively; love of the Spouse for her Head is related in the royal poems, while hope of the Church Militant is in the prayers of trust; and, anticipation of the glory of the Church Triumphant is apparent in the thanksgiving songs and the songs of the Kingdom.

It is, therefore, not necessary personally to feel all the sentiments expressed by the texts. It would be useless, even impossible, to spend the greater part of our lives in mourning and in weeping as the sick man, the persecuted, and the oppressed. But we intercede for our brothers who suffer, and they are many, in the name of the Church which supplies in its members the sorrowful Passion of Christ. The words of Jesus (Jn. 12:8), amplified and explained, are verified in the passage of centuries: "The poor, the accused, the persecuted, the sick, the sinners, you have always with you . . . ." Thanks to a wonderful gift of tongues, we all speak the language of the wretched[19] and, in the thanksgivings, the tongue of every sort of happiness as well. Some of the Psalms in which tortured souls confess their anguish, even more their despair (88), give us the opportunity to share the intellectual and moral distress under which certain of our contemporaries labor as they look haltingly for God (Acts 17:27).

[19]Pss. 17, 29, 31, 45, 66, 117, 123, 137.

Canonical and Personal Prayer. The Psalms are admirably adapted to the public prayer of the Church, for their authors, even in individual supplications, always intervene as members of the community of the Covenant. Their frequent passage from "I" to "We" is in no way disconcerting to men of our time who possess a feeling for the communal aspect of salvation. Besides, canonical prayer does not suppress personal prayer; rather, canonical prayer instructs, directs, stimulates, and protects it against wandering without a guide.[20]

Specialized Prayers. Some exegetes, persuaded that the greater part of the Psalms had their origin in worship and were destined for the liturgy, point out their precise role in the festivities of the Temple. They were used for the solemnity marking the enthronement of the divine King; the annual celebration of the choice of Sion and the Davidic dynasty; the ceremony of the renewal of the Covenant; and the liturgy of Yahwist fidelity.[21] These are more or less well-founded hy-

[20]Cf. J. A. Jungmann, "Sens et problèmes du culte," *Nouvelle Revue Theólogique*, LXXXII (1960), 823-39.

[21]Readers interested in this liturgical problem, which is hotly debated at the present day, may consult the following works: Sigmund Mowinckel, *The Psalms in Israel's Worship*, trans. David R. Ap-Thomas (Nashville, Tenn.: Abingdon Press, 1962), I, pp. 106-92; Artur Weiser, *The Psalms*, trans. Herbert Wartwell, (Philadelphia: The Westminster Press, 1962) pp. 35-62; Giorgio Castellino, *Libro dei Salmi* (Turin: Marietti, 1955), pp. 65-77. A summary of current trends and problems in exegesis can be found in *L'Ami du Clergé*, LXXIII (1963), 65-77.

potheses. The present headings of the Psalter show, in any case, that the Israelite community recited or sang certain Psalms on the occasion of special feasts (91; 23 and 93 in the Septuagint, as well as 29, 37, 69, and the group 119-133).

Today, the Church makes special use of a number of prayers by bringing them into relation with the different mysteries of Christ, commemorated and made present in worship.[22] Thus, Psalms 79 and 84 are characteristic of the season of Advent; Psalms 2, 97, and 109 of Christmas time; Psalms 65 and 71 of Epiphany week; Psalms 31, 50, and 129 recur again and again during Lent; Psalms 68 and 87 are in harmony with the sorrow of the Passion. During Holy Week we meditate on Psalms 21, 26, and 141; at Easter, the Church draws our attention to Psalms 15 and 29; at the Ascension to Psalms 23 and 46; and at Pentecost to Psalms 47 and 67. This pedagogy, in conformity with the tradition of the Fathers, introduces us to a method of bringing the Psalms into our daily life by placing Christ "always living to make intercession for us" (Heb. 7:25) at the center of the Psalms. There is a well-known axiom stating that we recite every Psalm "of Christ," "to Christ," or "in Christ." In short, the use of the Psalter in community does away with a rugged individualism without any harm to the personal character of prayer.

[22]Cf. Mgr. Garrone, *Psaumes et Prière* (Paris: Casterman, 1952), pp. 46-94.

Conclusion: Cultivating One's Soul

The painstaking application of these directives will not automatically produce wonderful effects. Intimacy with God results neither from knowledge nor from skill or art. Prayer bubbles up from the depths of the soul. All the erudition of the exegete and the historian, the ingenuity of the translator, the melodies of composer, and the competence of the liturgist will not succeed in fanning that mysterious spark that is authentically supernatural prayer. However, with God's help all these preparatory efforts contribute to forging a soul in us—a biblical soul, capable of firmly grasping the permanent spiritual resources of Jewish prayer. Yet, it is a Christian soul which, while sensible to the prophetic values of the Psalms, is penetrated with the newness and the transforming dynamism of the Gospel. Such a soul is visited by the Spirit and made ready to say anew, as they should be said anew, the words which he has breathed forth. To bring the Psalms to life, he who prays them must be alive. The Psalter does not give us readymade prayers, but offers us prayers to make.

PART 2
The Psalms in Their Literary Types

[4]

O Lord, Cure Me

Our sufferings, whatever form they take, are set before us in the Psalter. We hear there the echo, often a poignant one, of the manifold and varied distress that afflicts all mankind in this vale of tears. This celebrated description in the *Hail! Holy Queen* is itself derived from a Psalm (83:7, Vg.). The psalmists moan a great deal and often weep. The individual laments by themselves make up one-fourth of the total collection of Psalms, a considerable proportion. Men mourn more often than they celebrate. In the pitiable procession of the unhappy, we notice representatives of different social classes, young and old, kings and leaders, priests, Levites, and wise men. And sorrow wears many masks: those of the accused, prisoners, exiles, the persecuted, sinners, and the poor. The impressive number of sick people attracts our attention first.

The Psalter of the Sick

It is almost impossible to draw accurately and with any certainty a complete catalog of prayers of the sick. The list differs in length as different commentators draw it up. These variations are easily understandable. Often, as a matter of fact, the designation of those who mourn remains unclear, for the persecuted mainly portray their anguish in images drawn from sickness, while those who are sick generally describe their pains in terms of persecution. Still others undergo the attacks of physical suffering and the assaults of their adversaries at the same time. When account has been taken of these differences, we can still identify about twenty laments as outpourings of the sick.[1] In the Roman Breviary, these Psalms are spread throughout the days of the week, except Sunday. The Church carries remembrance of her suffering members in her daily prayer.

When one of the faithful fell sick, he spontaneously turned toward his only Savior. But Asa, sick from head to foot, did not consult Yahweh, but doctors. There are some circles who blame the use of healers as a lack of faith. The remark in Chronicles (2 Par. 16:12) sounds like a reproach. That may have been because medical activity was considered to be in competition with the omnipotence of God. At that time, medicine may have been more or less contaminated with magic. Some undoubtedly suspected the medical practitioner of conniving with occult powers. Ben Sirach, a man of faith, good sense, and humor reconciled these apparently contradictory aspects: "My son, when you are ill, delay not, but pray to God who will heal you: flee

[1]Pss. 6, 12, 21, 24(?), 27; 30:10-25; 37, 38; 39:14-18; 40, 68, 69, 70, 85(?), 87; 101:11-12; 108, 142. Cf. Is. 38:9-20; Lam. 3.

wickedness; let your hands be just, cleanse your heart of every sin; offer your sweet-smelling oblation in petition, a rich offering according to your means." This is the spiritual commandment and treatment according to reason: "Then give the doctor his place lest he leave; for you need him too. There are times that give him an advantage, and he too beseeches God that his diagnosis may be correct and his treatment bring about a cure" (Sir. 38:9-14).

With the Psalter's help, some elements of the supernatural practice of medicine can be divined: the sick man puts on a garment of haircloth or a mourning robe (29:12). He mortifies his soul, that is to say, gives himself over to fasting and pours himself forth in supplication (34:13-14), with his hands stretched toward the sanctuary (27:2). If possible, he goes up to the Temple to recite the prayer of an afflicted one when he is faint, and draws out his anguish before the Lord (101:1). This ceremony provided, in particular, for rites of expiation: the confession of sins (31:5) and sprinkling or ablution (50:9). The oracle of salvation or the priestly blessing brought comfort to the afflicted one. Here is an example of a sick man's Psalm:

> O Lord, reprove me not in your anger,
>   nor chastise me in your wrath.
> Have pity on me, O Lord, for I am languishing;
> Heal me, O Lord, for my body is in terror;
> My soul, too, is utterly terrified;
>   but you, O Lord, how long . . . ?
> Return, O Lord, save my life;
> Rescue me because of your kindness,

For among the dead no one remembers you;
  in the nether world who gives you thanks?
I am wearied with sighing;
Every night I flood my bed with weeping;
I drench my couch with my tears.
My eyes are dimmed with sorrow;
  they have aged because of all my foes.
Depart from me, all evildoers,
For the Lord has heard the sound of my weeping;
The Lord has heard my pleas;
  the Lord has accepted my prayer.
All my enemies shall be put to shame in utter terror;
  they shall fall back in sudden shame. (6:2-11)

Structure of the Prayers

The usual structure of a prayer of this sort is first a vehement outcry, prolonged in a suppliant complaint, and closing with a promise of thanksgiving. The development follows a measured plan in four divisions: invocation, presentation of the situation, plea, and assertion of the certainty of being heard. This arrangement permits some changes. The poet adds, omits, intermingles, inverts, or repeats. Although a lyrical outpouring never obeys rigid rules, the same essential lines are found with more or less precision. Today's liturgical editions quite properly underline these key articulations by the use of typographical devices. Some supplications seem spontaneous, issuing from experience, and composed at the very moment of suffering. Others, *centos* of clichés and all-purpose formulae, probably come from the keepers of the Temple. Clerics composed these general statements for the use of faithful souls who gathered at the sanctuary to ask for a cure.

The Invocation. From the very first words, an urgent invocation sets the tone: the sick man launches an appeal for help. He calls upon his Savior by name: "O Lord . . . O Lord of armies . . . my God . . . O Lord, my God . . . God of Israel." This recourse to the "name" was to give impetus to supernatural power for, according to the ancients, the name, so to speak, took in the person. The psalmist, son of the Covenant, addressed himself to God in the imperative accents of an ultimatum: "Save me! (68:2) . . . Have pity on me . . . Cure me! (6:2-3) . . . answer me speedily! (101:3) . . . how long will you hide your face from me?" (12:2; 37:2.) This bold lack of ceremony, these importune and impatient summonses, imitated by the sick people in the Gospel, are nothing less than wonderful acts of faith in the power and goodness of the Lord, who is always near and active, just and compassionate.

Lament. Invocation is followed by the lament, the characteristic part of every Psalm of this type. In order to enlist the pity of the Savior and to speed his intervention, the sick man lays bare his sorrowful condition. He adopts the tactics of the beggar. The most eloquent language of the barefoot beggar consists in showing himself with his haggard visage, ragged beard, and tattered clothing. The sick man shows himself in detail, boldly, with insistence, verve, and exaggeration. As is customary among the men of the Near East, he bares his physical and social breakdown and his moral anguish.

PHYSICAL BREAKDOWN. Sickness distorts the whole human being—his flesh, bone, and "soul." It affects the principal organs—heart, kidneys, and eyes. It further is characterized by the most alarming symptoms: lack of appetite, gradual loss of weight, weakness, fever, a bent-over back, trembling, piercing pains, purulent wounds and abscesses, lack of sleep, night sweats, and untimely old age. The descriptions given, while less detailed and wordy than those found in the Babylonian lamentations, sometimes allow ingenious commentators to diagnose the nature of the sickness, whether it be leprosy, paralysis, the plague, some other contagious infection (30:12; 37:6 ff.; 87:9 ff.), or merely extreme weakness accompanied by fever (21:15 ff.). It is risky to make a precise diagnosis, for metaphors and hyperboles must be taken into account. A prayer does not go into the same sort of detail as a medical report, but those who suffer will recognize something other than mere literature in the following descriptions. "There is no health in my flesh . . . no wholeness in my bones . . . noisome and festering are my sores . . . I am steeped and bowed down profoundly . . . I am numbed and severely crushed . . . my heart throbs . . . my strength forsakes me; the very life of my eyes has failed me" (37:4, 6, 7-8, 11). "I am wearied with calling, my throat is parched, my eyes have failed" (68:4). "Like a lengthening shadow I pass away; I am swept away like the locust. My knees totter from my fasting, and my flesh is waster of its substance" (128:23-24). "Have pity on me, O Lord, for I am in distress; with sorrow my eye is consumed; my soul also and my body. For my life is spent with grief and my years with sighing; my strength has failed to affliction, and my bones are consumed" (30:10-11). "For my days vanish like smoke, and my bones burn like fire. Withered and dried up like grass is my heart; I forget to eat my bread. Because of my insistent sighing I am reduced to skin and bone. I am like a desert owl; I have become like an owl among the rulers. I am sleepless and I moan; I am like a sparrow alone on the housetop" (101:4-8). "I am like water poured out; all my bones are wracked. My heart has become like wax melting away within my bosom. My throat is dried up like baked clay, my tongue cleaves to my jaws" (21:15-16).

LONELINESS: ABANDONMENT BY FRIENDS AND NEIGHBORS. Loneliness weighs heavily upon the sick man condemned to live differently and apart: "I am imprisoned and I cannot escape" (87:9). Indifference, forgetfulness, and abandonment by his friends aggravate the trial of isolation. They torture sensitive hearts, which ill health renders particularly vulnerable: "You have taken my friends away from me; you have made me an abomination to them" (87:9). "For all my faults I am an object of reproach, the laughing stock of my neighbors, and a dread to my friends; they who see me abroad flee from me. I am forgotten like the unremembered dead; I am like a dish that is broken!" (30:12-13). "My friends and my companions stand back because of my affliction; my neighbors stand afar off" (37:12). "I have become an outcast to my brothers, a stranger to my mother's sons" (68:9). This is the very pinnacle of affliction: those who should be near stand apart.

Sometimes the sick man receives visitors. Unfortunately, they sharpen his pain instead of easing it. It is truly a difficult art for the healthy to feel in communion with the sick. "I looked for sympathy, but there was none; for comforters and I found none" (68:21). The wretched interprets silence, reticence, and commonplace conversation badly. Even in comforting words he smells hypocrisy and sometimes he is not wrong. "When one comes to see me, he speaks without sincerity; his heart stores up malice; when he leaves he gives voice to it outside" (40:7). Here is one utterance among others: "A malignant disease fills his frame." And to this diagnosis is added a stern foresight: "Now that he lies ill, he will not rise again" (40:9).

Friendship does not hold out for long when ill fortune strikes. The table companion, the confidant of the night before, betrays the unfortunate man; the ingrate changes alliances. "Even my friend who had my trust and partook of my bread, has raised his heel against me" (40:10). His enemies, for their part, relish the bad luck as a victory. The disgrace of their adversary fills them with joy. It is the source of their victory. They make merry, wink their eyes, wag their heads, gnash their teeth, mock, and deliver ironic and insulting comments: "My enemies say the worst of me: 'When will he die and his name perish?'" (40:6.)

"Yet when I stumbled they were glad and gathered together" (34:15, 19, 24, etc.).

PERSECUTION BY ENEMIES. A group of "enemies" moves about the sick man. Texts to this effect abound, and they intrigue us. We wonder who these personages were, so cruel in word and deed, who besieged sick people. The Psalms allude to these enemies. They bear different names, but specific references are extremely vague: "those who hate me . . . those who seek my ruin . . . those who detest me without cause . . . those who return evil for my good . . . my enemies . . . my opponents . . . my oppressors . . . those who rise up against me . . . the abettors of iniquity." Various metaphors depict their baneful activity. They are compared to warriors (108:3), to hunters with nets and snares (37:13), to wild beasts thirsty for blood, to lions, lionesses, bulls, buffaloes, and dogs (21:14; 34:21). Since there is no precise designation, the question of how this anonymity can be pierced remains.

In reality, these names and figures of speech correspond to different classes of men. The first group is made up of a circle that includes neighbors, friends, and intimates. These people, only yesterday of good will, today turn away from a man whom the Lord has stricken.[2] Sickness, because it was also considered punishment, singles out the unfortunate man as a sinner.[3] It was in that context that the friends of Job

[2]Pss. 30:12-13; 37:12; 40:10; 87:9.
[3]Pss. 38:12; 40:5; 106:17.

interpreted his maladies and misfortunes. Those devout men thought they were doing a pious deed by joining in with the divine judgment. They were modeling their behavior on that of an avenging God.

A second group brings together a band of skeptics, detractors of divine Providence. These free thinkers made merry over the disappointments of a practicing Jew, who was ill paid for his devotion. Certain complaints of the psalmists allow these sarcasms to be divined. "Because zeal for your house consumes me, and the insults of those who blaspheme you fall upon me. I humble myself with fasting, and this was made a reproach to me. I made sackcloth my garment, and I became a byword for them. They who sit at the gate gossip about me, and drunkards make me the butt of their songs" (68:10-13). "All who see me scoff at me; they mock me with parted lips, and they wag their heads: 'He relied on the Lord; let Him deliver him, let Him rescue him, if He loves him'" (21:8-9). "They who repay evil for good harass me for pursuing good" (37:21).

A third class seems rather well defined. They are the people who, even before his illness, had picked a quarrel with the psalmist. There had already existed quarrels and accounts to be paid off between them. When misfortune intervened, it was a windfall. These rancorous and quibbling characters threw themselves upon the unfortunate man like flies on a wound: "They kept after him whom you smote, added to the pain of him you wounded" (68:27). "For my enemies speak against me, and they who keep watch against my life take counsel together. They say, 'God has forsaken him; pursue and seize him, for there is no one to rescue him'" (70:10-11). "Unjust witnesses have risen up; things I knew not of, they lay to my charge" (34:11). "Must I restore what I did not steal?" (68:5.) The old enemies profit from the occasion and redouble their opposition to settle their differences. Hence, the judicial prosecutions, the calumnious accusations, the restraint on property, etc. In every raw, harsh society the weak must suffer!

In some cases,[4] the link between enemies and illness appears so closely intertwined that it may be rightly asked whether or not the sickness was caused by evil machinations. Some exegetes offer the hypothesis of magical incantations and sorcerers' charms. To be sure, the official religion proscribed witches, but we are by no means sure that this prohibition was always observed.

In any case, the Jews believed in the efficacy of curses and readily attributed this sort of evildoing to their enemies. They parried with the same poisoned weapons: "He loved cursing; may it come upon him; he took no delight in blessing: may it be far from him. And may he be clothed with cursing as with a robe; may it penetrate into his entrails like water and like oil into his bones; may it be for him like a garment which covers him, like a girdle which is always about

[4]Pss. 12:5; 27:3-5; 30:18-19, 21; 40:6-9; 108.

him" (108:17-19). A sick man complains of those "who in their rage against me make a curse of me" (101:9).

The Jews were ignorant of the immediate causes of certain physiological phenomena. Without denying the action of secondary causes, nonetheless they had no precise knowledge of them. In their eyes, existence in the here below was like a battlefield on which powers, favorable or inimical to life, collided mysteriously. The latter were at work day and night. A psalmist calls these demoniac forces to mind when he enumerates "the pestilence that roams in the darkness, the devastating plague at noon, the terror of the night and the arrow that flies by day" (90:5-6).

While curses, whispers of lying and insolent tongues, the "breath" of the abettors of iniquity are always present, who can say that they unleash the intervention of evil forces? Some may have assumed this, as even today Christians attribute the evils which weigh them down to "lots" cast against them by wicked neighbors. Jews, whether victims of real or imaginary curses, came to the Temple and called upon the Lord to neutralize the malign influences and to return them to their unjust persecutors. In virtue of the law of an eye for an eye, "let them curse, but do you bless!" (108:28.)

GOD'S SILENCE. Besides being abandoned by his friends and attacked by his enemies, the sick man complains further that he is apparently forsaken by the Lord. His partner in the Covenant plays dead, turns his back, or is silent. This impression of indifference drives the sick man to a paroxysm of anguish: "How long, O Lord? Will you utterly forget me? How long will you hide your face from me?" (12:2; cf. 89:13.) "My God, My God, why have you forsaken me? Far from my prayer, far from the words of my cry? O my God, I cry out by day, and you answer not; by night, and there is no relief for me" (21:2-3). The prayers come to a conclusion either without a ray of hope (87), or end in melancholy pessimism, even disillusionment, in the fashion of Job's complaints: "Turn your gaze from me, that I may find respite ere I depart and be no more" (38:14).

Some of the psalmists considered their illness as an anticipated death: "For my soul is surfeited with troubles and my life draws near to the nether world. I am numbered with those who go down into the pit; I am a man without strength. My couch is among the dead, like the slain who lie in the grave . . . in the bottom of the pit, in the dark abyss, down in the pit" (87:4-7; 142:3, 7). "The waters threaten my life; I am sunk in the abysmal swamp where there is no foothold; I have reached the watery depths; the flood overwhelms me" (68:2-3). The nether world has already seized its prey. That is why a cure is likened to an escape from the grave, to an ascent from the abyss, or an emergence from the underground waters, in short, to a return to life. Recovering one's health is a return to life.

Supplication. The prayers, prepared in the invocation, lay beneath the lament. Now it breaks forth in the supplication properly so-called: "Return, O Lord, save my life; rescue me because of your kindness" (6:5). "Give light to my eyes that I may not sleep in death" (12:4). "But you, O Lord, have pity on me, and raise me up" (40:11). "Rescue me out of the mire; may I not sink! May I be rescued . . . from the watery depths. Let not the flood-waters overwhelm me, nor the abyss swallow me up, nor the pit close its mouth over me" (68:15-16). "You will again revive me; from the depths of the earth you will once more raise me" (70:20). "O my God take me not hence in the midst of my days" (101:25). "Drag me not away with the wicked" (27:3). The sick, to persuade the Lord to intervene as soon as possible, urged, with a frequently pathetic insistence, using the same reasons although in different forms: "Cure me, for you care; it is to your interest; justice demands it; I confess my sin which has angered you; my life is so short!"

YOU CAN CURE ME! This fundamental argument, illustrated by Israel's history, is inscribed in the very heart of the Law. Life, as death, depends on the Lord: "I, the Lord, am your healer" (Ex. 15:26). . . . "It is I who bring both death and life, I who inflict wounds and heal them" (Dt. 32:39; cf. 7:15; 28:27, 60). . . . "He [the Lord] heals all your ills" (102:3). The psalmist presses God to retract his decision. He has stricken and wounded (68:27), scourged with blows, laid on his hand (38:11), sunk deep his arrows

(37:3), sent dread and terror (87:16-17), raised up and let fall (101:11). Let him now undo what he has done.

IT IS TO HIS INTEREST. If the sick man stumbles and falls, his "fall" into the pit deprives God of praises. In Sheol, land of forgetfulness and of silence, there are no more songs, no thanksgiving, and no liturgy. "Among the dead no one remembers you; in the nether world, who gives you thanks?" (6:6). . . "What gain would there be from my lifeblood, from my going down into the grave? Would dust give you thanks or proclaim your faithfulness?" (20:10). . . Will you work wonders for the dead? Will the shades arise to give you thanks? Do they declare your kindness in the grave, your faithfulness among those who have perished? Are your wonders made known in the darkness, or your justice in the land of oblivion?" (87:11-13; cf. Is. 38:18-19.)

JUSTICE DEMANDS IT. Injustice itself calls for a speedy rescue. The Lord, in virtue of the Covenant, guarantees the well-being and the life of his faithful. He owes it to himself to reward the just man and to hold him up when he makes a false step: "In the day of misfortune, the Lord will deliver him. The Lord will keep and preserve him: . . . the Lord will help him on his sick bed, he will take away all his ailments when he is ill" (40:2-4). It is impossible for the just judge to treat the good and the wicked alike: "Drag me not away with the wicked, with those who do wrong" (27:3). "The evildoers will not live out half their days" (54:24), but will die a premature death. This is their normal reward. The Lord will tear down the wicked man and he will not rebuild him (27:5); he will wipe him out from the book of the living and he will not inscribe him with the just men (68:29). Any other attitude may be set down to inadvertence, to sleepiness, or to forgetfulness. It provokes scandal and disappointment of the good (38:3, 10); and, in the long run, the derision of the wicked and foolish (38:9).

I CONFESS MY SIN. Not all of the sick are so sure of their righteousness. Sometimes they feel themselves sinners before God, and therefore liable to punishment. "Before God no living man is just" (142:2). "Chastise me not in your wrath" (6:2; 37:2). Thus, they implore pardon and healing at once. The confession, in their thought, disarms the divine executioner: "O Lord, have pity on me! Cure me! I have sinned against thee" (40:5). . . . "Indeed, I acknowledge my guilt; I grieve over my sin" (37:19). "A sick man regrets his foolishness and his failures. He puts on the sackcloth of mourning, breaks his soul by fasting" (68:6,11-12). Another, after his cure, draws this lesson from his experience: "As long as I would not speak, my bones wasted away with my groaning all the day, for day and night your hand was heavy upon me; my strength was dried up as by the heat of summer. Then I acknowledged my sin to you, my guilt I covered not. I said, 'I confess my faults to the Lord,' and you took away the guilt of my sin" (31:3⁻5).

LIFE IS SO SHORT. One last motive cannot fail to touch the Eternal: the shortness and fragility of man's existence: "I am afflicted and in agony from my youth" (87:16). . . . "A short span you have made my days, and my life is as naught before you; only a breath is any human existence. A phantom only, man goes his ways; like vapor only are his restless pursuits; . . . Take away your scourge from me; at the blow of your hand I wasted away. With rebukes for guilt you chasten man; you dissolve like a cobweb all that is dear to him. Only a breath is any man . . . for I am but a wayfarer before you, a pilgrim like all my fathers" (38:6-7,11-12, 13). Here is the very voice of Ecclesiastes.

Assurance of Being Heard. Almost always, at the end of the prayer, a lightning flash crosses the night. The whole tone changes suddenly. There is no longer invocation, lament, nor supplication, but only the joyous certainty of being heard and the hint of a thanksgiving or its promise. "The Lord has heard my plea; the Lord has accepted my prayer" (6:9-10). A psalmist, more than impatient when he began (12:2-3), ends his plea in complete calm: "Let me sing of the Lord, He has been good to me" (12:7).

Another, haunted by imminent death (27:1), closes in joy: "Blessed be the Lord, for he has heard the sound of my pleading" (27:6). The psalmist sketches[5] and sometimes develops a song of gratitude (21:23

[5]Pss. 12:7; 27:7-8; 34:28; 68:31-32; 70:22-24; 108:30.

ff.; 30:20 ff.). It is thanksgiving to God the Savior, a public profession of faith and, for the community, an invitation to try the goodness and the faithfulness of God. The pleader is changed into an apostle.

We may well ask what is the cause that justifies this sudden about-face, this sudden bursting forth into joy. It may be faith fed on prayer and raised by it. Or, perhaps the suppliant has discerned some sign of a favorable answer upon which he counts heavily.[6] A priest may even have risen in the assembly to utter an oracle of salvation. Some exegetes suppose that the Psalms of distress were given an ending only after they were heard, and then deposited in the temple as *ex-votos*. That is how these Psalms began their liturgical existence. Then, they were at the disposition of other sick people, and also, perhaps, at the disposition of others who had been cured of their ills.

OUR PRAYER

Sick people are found in every part of the world. Those who are ill today recognize themselves in the descriptions of their forerunners. There is nothing essential to be modified. If some details must be accented, others are blurred to fit the individual case. The community of suffering finds a kinship especially within the soul. Even in an age of medicine and surgery, the cry to God spontaneously bursts forth from hearts in pain. The sciences, in spite of their rapid strides, come up short against limits and reach the end of

[6]Cf. 12:4; 21:3; 37:16; 68:14, 17, 18.

their powers. In addition to its biological aspect, sickness takes on a religious meaning. Even from this point of view, the Christian is the beneficiary of an added light, but his psychology in infirmity does not coincide exactly with that of the psalmist. The situations are alike, but that is not to say they are the same.

The moral make up of the Jews of long ago was necessarily bound to the religious and social context of their time (an exclusively earthly retribution, e.g., the predominant concept of sickness as punishment, the efficacy of curses, and the law of an eye for an eye and a tooth for a tooth). The Christian draws back these curtains in his prayer. He knows that faith does not immunize the believer against physical trials, and so he breaks the bond between suffering and sin. Sickness for him is not necessarily the punishment of personal sin (Jn. 9:2-3), but rather attests the presence of sin in the world (Gn. 3:8; Rom. 8:18 ff.), while possessing an expiatory and redemptive value. Finally, for the Christian, life here below does not end in a ghostly existence in Sheol, but opens to an eternity of glory: "For thy faithful, O Lord, life is changed and not taken away; if the dwelling of our earthly sojourn is destroyed, a heavenly habitation is prepared for us in the heavens." Physical death, however untimely, is not the supreme catastrophe.

The prayers of sick people are not reserved for the ill alone. In the unity of solidarity of the Mystical Body of Christ, those who are well intercede for the stricken members. The suggestions of the Gospel invite us even to place this sort of supplication on the lips of the Lord, patient and burdened with every sort of wretchedness. These descriptions, taken as a whole, serve to express the essential feelings and also to convey his Passion and prayer. This transfer brings a total renewal. The suffering of Christ is original in its courses, its reality, and its effects. On the other hand, the inner attitude of the Son of God, the redeemer of men, infinitely surpasses the experience of the psalmists. Finally, we may lawfully accommodate these same formulae to imploring health for the soul. Jeremiah was not ill when he used the language of the sick.[7] "Heal me, Lord, that I may be healed; save me, that I may be saved, for it is you whom I praise" (Jer. 17:14; cf. the capitulum of Terce for Tuesday). Each day, the liturgy of the Mass exhorts us to ask for spiritual strength by likening ourselves to the sick: "Speak but the word and my soul will be healed" (*Dic verbo et sanabitur anima mea*). Jesus, healer and

[7]Charles Hauret, "Note d'exégèse, Jérémie XVII, 14. Sana me, Domine, et sanabor," *Revue des Sciences Religieuses*, XXXVI (1962), 178-84.

savior, heals the wounds of the body and the sickness of the soul together (Mt. 9:1-8).[8]

[8]Cf. André Feuillet, "Souffrance et confiance en Dieu. Commentaire du Psaume 22 (21)," *Nouvelle Revue Théologique*, LXX (1948), 137-49; Hilaire Duesberg, *Le Psautier des malades* (Maredsous: Éditions de Maredsous, 1952); Albert Gelin, "Les quatres lectures du Psaume XXII (21)," *Bible et Vie chrétienne*, I (1953), 31-39 (English trans., *The Poor of Yahweh*, trans. Kathryn Sullivan [Collegeville, Minnesota: The Liturgical Press, 1964], pp. 82-90); Robert Martin-Achard, "La prière d'un malade: quelques remarques sur le psaume 38 (37)," *Verbum Caro*, XLV (1958), 77-82; Evode Beaucamp, "Guérison et pardon, Ps. 103 (102)," *Bible et Vie chrétienne*, XXIX (1959), 13-25; G. Pidoux, *La main qui guérit. Psaumes du malade* (Neuchâtel:Delachaux et Niestlé, 1960); R. Swaeles, "Le thème biblique: Celui qui vient pour nous guérir," and Ph. Rouillard, "Le Christ vient guérir les hommes," *Assemblées du Seigneur* (Bruges:Publications de Saint André, Éditions Biblica, 1961), IV, pp. 51-80; "Maladie-Guérison," Xavier Léon-Dufour *et al.*, editors, *Vocabulaire de Théologie Biblique* (Paris: Éditions du Cerf, 1962), cols. 566-570.

[5]

Judge Me, Defend My Cause

A general impression emerges from the greater part of the Psalms of distress. In Israel, men led a rough and dangerous existence, a true struggle for life. We do not always succeed in uncovering the precise difficulties against which the psalmists struggled. But besides the sick, several classes of persecuted—particularly exiles and those accused of crime—may be classified with some probability. Still, we should avoid giving too much rigidity to these classifications.

PSALMS OF THE ACCUSED

The Judgment of God. In ancient times, justice was rendered at the gate of the town (126:5) which was, so to speak, the public square. But, in certain disputes (Dt. 17:8; 19:16), the accused was hailed before the religious authorities. At times, to justify himself, one so charged called upon the judgment of God. Solomon, in his prayer at the dedication of the Temple, mentions this extraordinary procedure: "If a man sin against his neighbor, and an oath be laid upon him compelling him to swear, and he come and swear before thine

82

altar in this house, then hear thou in the heavens; take action and judge thy servants, punishing the wicked by bringing his course of action upon his own head, and vindicating the righteous by rewarding him according to his righteousness" (3 Kgs. 8:31-32).

This custom, also known among the ancient Arabs, was practiced in Israel for a long time (Ex. 22:7-10; cf. Ex. 23:7).

Accusers and the accused appeared together before God, the supreme judge (1 Sm. 2:25). How the process unfolded is unknown. Doubtless it was made up (Dt. 6; 21:1-9; Nm. 5:11 ff.) of different ritual acts, sacrifice, washing, prayers, and recourse to the divine name (Dt. 6:13; cf. Ps. 62:12). The taking of an oath, with or without a conditional curse, constituted of itself a sufficient proof of innocence, so much were the effects of perjury feared (Ex. 20:7). A man might lie to men, but he could not deceive God.

Protestations of Innocence. Some Psalms,[1] placed in this particular context, take on fresh meaning: They must have served as justifying formulae. Some exegetes add to their number,[2] relying on often questionable signs, for it may well have been that the ancient procedure of divine judgment simply influenced and colored the terminology of the psalmists.

[1]Pss. 5, 7, 16, 25, 26:7-14; 34, 138 (?), 141.
[2]Pss. 4, 10, 12, 30, 53, 54, 55, 56, 58, 93.16-23; 108, 139.

RECOURSE TO THE SUPREME TRIBUNAL. Here is a man, very probably a priest, harassed by those who calumniate him. He hastens to the Temple, his refuge, and prepares a sacrifice. He pronounces his prayer; then, trustingly, looks for the Lord's answer: "Heed my call for help, my king and my God! To you I pray, O Lord; at dawn you hear my voice; at dawn I bring my plea expectantly before you" (5:3-4).

Other psalmists appear even more insistent: "O Lord, my God, in you I take refuge; save me from all my persecutors and rescue me, lest I become like the lion's prey to be torn to pieces, with no one to rescue me" (7:2-3). "Fight, O Lord, against those who fight me; war against those who make war on me. Take up the shield and buckler, and rise up in my defense. Brandish the lance, and block the way in the face of my pursuers; say to my soul, 'I am your salvation'" (34:1-3). "Do me justice, O Lord!" (25:1.) So the divine tribunal, court of last instance, has the case before it.

PLEADING OF THE DEFENDANT. The simple pleading was ordinarily made up of praise for the impartial and well-informed Judge: "Judge of the nations . . . just judge" . . . (7:9). "No evil man remains with you. The arrogant may not stand in your sight. You hate all evildoers; you destroy all who speak falsehood" (5:5-7) . . . "Protector of those who love your name" (5:13; 7:10) . . . "Shield of the upright of heart" (7:11). "Searcher of the heart and soul (7:10; 16:3; 25:2; cf. 138:23) . . . "all-knowing and incorruptible witness" (34:22; 138). Then, in the presence of God,

who was on the judge's seat to hand down the sentence
(7:7-8), the accused faithful asserts his innocence of
the charges uttered against him. Then follows his
proclamation of righteousness. It is comparable to the
negative confessions of the Assyro-Babylonians and
Egyptians because he claims neither sinlessness nor
entire innocence, but rejects the charge as unwarrant-
ed. On this precise point, he pleads not guilty: "O
Lord, my God, if I am at fault in this, if there is guilt
on my hands . . . let the enemy pursue and overtake
me" (7:4-6). Convinced of his innocence, he recalls
his irreproachable conduct (16:4-5; cf. 138:21-22) and
declares himself ready to submit to ordeal: "Though
you test my heart, searching it in the night, though
you try me with fire" (16:3; 25:2; 138:23) . . . "do
me justice, O Lord, because I am just" (7:9). . . .
"Your presence, O Lord, I seek" (26:8) . . . "from
you let my judgment come; your eyes behold what is
right" (16:2).

ATTACK AGAINST HIS ACCUSERS. The attack against
his adversaries follows his defense. The unflattering
portrait of his enemies, heavy with rather conventional
details, is frequent in the Wisdom writings: "In their
mouth there is no sincerity: their heart teems with
treacheries. Their throat is an open grave; they flatter
with their tongue" (5:10); "They shut up their cruel
hearts, their mouths speak proudly" (16:10). "On
their hands are crimes, and their right hands are full
of bribes" (25:10). . . . "He who has conceived iniquity and was pregnant with mischief, brings forth

failure" (7:15). . . . "Without cause they set their
snare for me, without cause they dug a pit against
my life" (34:7; 7:16). "False witnesses have risen up
against me, and such as breathe out violence" (26:12).
. . . "Unjust witnesses have risen up; things I knew
not of, they lay to my charge" (34:11).

PRAYER AND TRUST IN GOD'S VERDICT. In conclusion, there was a solemn appeal to God's judgment:
"Rise up, O Lord, to judge me. . . . Give me not over
to the envy of my enemies. . . . Keep me as the apple
of thy eye, hide me in the shadow of thy wings . . .
awake! Rise up to defend my cause, judge me according to thy justice. . . . Bring me forth from prison!"[3]
With confidence and hope, the accused calmly awaits
the verdict: "Wait for the Lord with courage; be
stouthearted, and wait for the Lord" (26:14).

Many points remain obscure. It is impossible to
specify the titles of the arraignment (murder, theft,
idolatry, association with the wicked?) and thereby char-
acterize the nature of the trial imposed upon the defendant. It is also impossible to determine the manner
in which the Lord notifies him of his arrest. The
faithless denouncers, rejected and condemned, are subject, in virtue of the law of an eye for an eye and a
tooth for a tooth, to the punishment which they sought
for their victim: "They are ensnared in their own
snare" (7:16-17). The discharged defendant, snatched
from prison (141:8), sings of his joy in thanksgiving.[4]

[3]Pss. 7:7; 12:8; 26:12; 34:23; 141:8.
[4]Pss. 5:12-13; 7:18; 16:15; 26:14; 34:27-28; 141:8.

The use of these Psalms is not at all out of date. When unjustly accused, we can certainly affirm that it is an error, but we ought especially to have confidence in him who is the Lord and who one day or another will lay down his decision. To be sure, there is no excuse for employing the curses of the past. If we ourselves are not accused, let us remember that it is extremely grave and dangerous to casually make charges against others. In the case of a false accusation, it is to God himself that we must take ourselves. It is the Lord who binds his own cause to that of the "refugees" whom we incriminate. He will do justice speedily. But what we must not cease to remember is the trial of Christ. How characteristic it was that the false witnesses accused Christ when he was judged. In his Passion, Christ not only took up the words of the psalmists but, above all, their life, and, by the same token, the life of all of those unjustly condemned and held inferior or infamous.[5] Christian perfection—foolishness for the wise of this world—goes beyond the demands of strict justice (Mt. 5:10-12). It is ruled by norms unknown to the psalmists. More exactly, it is modeled on a Person (I Pt. 2:21-22).

PRAYERS OF THE EXILES

Lamentation. Homesickness for Jerusalem. The individual complaints of men banished, outlawed, and of the faithful in distant exile from the Temple, are of

[5]A. Maillot and A. Lelievre, *Les Psaumes* (Geneva: Labor et Fides, 1961), I, pp. 107-8.

great interest although small in number.[6] One who
has been deported prays from the *ends of the earth*
(60:33). Another lived in the midst of disloyal and
warlike people: "in Mosoch, among the tents of Cedar"
(119:5). The third lives in a desert land (according
to a variant in the text), on a soil "parched, lifeless,
and without water" (62:2). A priest or Levite, driven
off to the sources of the Jordan, in the region dominated by the peaks of Hermon (31:7), has left us a well-
known Psalm that furnishes the prayers at the foot of
the altar at Mass.

Exile brings ripeness to character. The things which
one is deprived of for the moment are better appre-
ciated. Far from their native hearth, the psalmists felt
homesickness, nostalgia for Jerusalem and for the rock
of Sion inaccessible to them (60:3). Their thoughts
were directed to the King, the Anointed of the Lord
(60:7-8; 62:12), toward the Temple where they shared
the lavish and joyful performance of liturgical ceremonies in better days (41:5; 60:5; 62:3). How inter-
minable time appeared to those without a country!
"All too long have I dwelt with those who hate peace"
(119:6).

THIRST FOR GOD. Trial whets the conscience and
refines the spiritual feeling of religious souls. When
the habitual supports of piety are lost, spirituality
gains in depth and direction. The Levite of Jordan,
without quite arriving at full worship in spirit, none-

[6]Pss. 41-42; 60, 62, 119 (?).

theless felt the thirst for God, a feeling that others
call the search for the Lord, the indispensable main-
spring of authentic religion: "As the hind longs for
the running waters, so my soul longs for you, O God.
Athirst is my soul for God, the living God. When
shall I go and behold the face of God? Those times
I recall now that I pour out my soul within me, when
I went with the throng and led them in procession to
the house of God, amid loud cries of joy and thanksgiving, with the multitude keeping festival" (41:2-3,5).
And here are other wonderful formulae, cleanly struck
like coats of arms: "For your kindness is a greater good
than life; . . . my soul clings fast to you" (62:4,9).
. . . "O God, you are my God whom I seek" (62:2).
. . . "O, that I might lodge in your tent forever, take
refuge in the shelter of your wings!" (60:5; 62:8.)

HOSTILITY OF THOSE ROUND ABOUT. The hostility
of one's own circle puts a keen edge on suffering, for
spiritual isolation weighs even heavier than material
distance alone. In these Psalms, as in other supplications, the enemies carry on the fight openly or secretly.[7]
"My foes mock me, as they say to me day after day,
'where is your God?'" (41:4, 11.) Sickness may have
been added to the tribulations of the exiled. Some ex-
pressions hint at this without proving it. The bread
of tears (41:4); the going about in mourning (41:10;
42:2); the crushing of bones (41:11); the floods and
the waves, comparable to the tumultuous torrents

[7]Pss. 41:11; 42:1-2; 60:4; 62:10; 119:2-3, 6-7.

which hurl themselves down in cascades on the slopes of Hermon (41:9), may all symbolize moral anguish.

Supplication. Neither inner anxiety nor the ill will caused by religious indifference of those close to the psalmist proved obstacles to the silence in the depths of his soul where the intimate presence of God and the dialogue of prayer continued both night and day (41:9; 62:7,9). In spite of passing spells of dejection, faith in the living God remained and, with it, fits and starts of hope. Present sorrow would soon give place to high glee: "Send forth your light and your fidelity; they shall lead me on and bring me to your holy mountain, to your dwelling place. Then will I go into the altar of God, the God of my gladness and joy; then will I give you thanks upon the harp, O God, my God! Why are you so downcast, O my soul? Why do you sigh within me? Hope in God! For I shall again be thanking him, in the presence of my savior and my God" (42:3-5). As always, in the darkest of shadows, salvation is seen on the horizon.

Christian Prayer. At Gethsemane, Jesus again repeats, it seems, the refrain of the exiled psalmist (Mt. 26:38; cf. Jn. 12:27). So many occasions to imitate his example are given us. There are only slight changes to be made. Surely, it is not our responsibility to condemn our detractors "to the edge of the sword, to the mouths of jackals" (62:11), nor to draw down on the head of aggressors "sharp arrows of a warrior with fiery coals of brushwood" (119:4) unfair as they seem.

We must let the Lord re-establish justice in his own fashion.

But the thirst for God, the primacy of praise (42:4; 62:5), the love for worship, and absolute trust in the midst of the trials of earthly existence do not represent exile for Christians: All these are so many permanent and indispensable religious values.[8]

LAMENT OF THE JUST MAN PERSECUTED

In the greater part of the Psalms of distress, there are no clear-cut allusions to illness, judicial prosecution, nor to exile; but there is frequent mention of persecutors. The psalmists lived in a climate of war and insecurity that gave their lives a tragic character.

Here is a typical prayer:

O God, by your name save me,
  and by your might defend my cause.
O God, hear my prayer;
  harken to the words of my mouth.
For haughty men have risen up against me,
And fierce men seek my life;
  they set not God before their eyes.
Behold, God is my helper;
  the Lord sustains my life.
Turn back the evil upon my foes;
  in your faithfulness destroy them.
Freely will I offer you sacrifice;
I will praise your name, O Lord, for its goodness,
  because from all distress you have rescued me,
  and my eyes look down upon my enemies. (53:3-9)

---

[8]A. Rose, "La soif du Dieu Vivant, Ps. 42-43 (41-42)," *Bible et Vie chrétienne*, XXV (1959), 29-38; "L'Autel du Seigneur," *ibid.*, XXVI (1960), 29-37.

Here is a Psalm of classical construction to be used in any necessity. First, there is a vague description of proud, violent enemies, careless of religion, whose intrigues plunge the just man into anguish. Then, the persecuted man calls upon the name of God, that is to say, the power of One joined to him in Covenant, who is always faithful and ready to act. Finally, divine intervention brings the adversary to naught and produces the expression of thanksgiving.

The Ravages of Evil in Society. Some lamentations[9] reflect a very somber contingency, a religious and social circle degraded to the extreme. Absence of faith fostered the boldness of the wicked and unleashed their appetites and the exploitation of the humble: ". . . in the city I see violence and strife; day and night they prowl about upon its walls. Evil and mischief are in its midst; (treachery is in its midst): Oppression and fraud never depart from its streets" (54:10-12). . . . "I lie prostrate in the midst of lions which devour men; their teeth are spears and arrows, their tongue is a sharp sword" (56:5). . . . "Each evening they return, they snarl like dogs and prowl about the city. They wander about as scavengers; if they are not filled, they howl" (58:7-8, 15-16) . . . "who sharpen their tongues like swords, who aim like arrows their bitter words, shooting from ambush at the innocent man, suddenly shooting at him without fear" (63:4-5). . . . "They

[9]Pss. 54, 55, 56, 58, 63, 139, 140.

make their tongues sharp as those of serpents; the venom of asps is under their lips" (139:4).

Corruption undermines the upper classes of society. A psalmist belabors the false leaders, obstinate in evil and insensible to what is right: "Do you indeed like gods pronounce justice and judge fairly, you men of rank? May you willingly commit crimes; on earth you look to the fruits of extortion. From the womb the wicked are perverted: astray from birth have the liars gone. Theirs is poison like the serpent, like that of a stubborn snake that stops its ears, that it may not hear the voice of enchanters casting cunning spells" (57:2-6; cf. 81:2-5).

This contagion does not spare the clergy. Defections occur in its ranks. This may be concluded with probability from the apostrophe of Psalm 54 against the faithless friends: "If an enemy had reviled me, I could have borne it; if he who hates me had vaunted himself against me, I might have hidden from him; But you, my other self, my companion and my bosom friend! You, whose comradeship I enjoyed; at whose side I walked in procession in the house of God! . . . Each one lays hands on his associates, and violates his pact. Softer than butter is his speech, but war is in his heart" (54:13-15, 21-22).

A keen glance at a society whose very foundations are crumbling (10:3) justifies pessimism: "Help, O Lord! for no one now is dutiful, faithfulness has vanished from among men. Everyone speaks falsehood to his neighbor; with smooth lips they speak, and double heart" (11:2-3); "The Lord looks down from heaven upon the children of men, to see if there be one who is wise and seeks God. All alike have gone astray; they have become perverse; there is not one who does good, not even one. They eat up my people just as they eat bread" (13:1-4; 52:3-5).

This corrupted and corrupting circle causes nausea and incites flight: "Had I but wings like a dove, I would fly away and be at rest. Far away I would flee; I would lodge in the wilderness. I would hasten to find shelter from the violent storm and the tempest" (54:7-9). While no solution is possible, one recourse at least remains: To pray *not* to come to agreement with evil and gain grace to escape universal contamination: "O Lord, set a watch before my mouth, a guard at the door of my lips. Let not my heart incline to the evil of engaging in deeds of wickedness with men who are evildoers; and let me not partake of their dainties" (140:3-4).

The Two "Cities." In these burning pages of the Psalter, the most diverse feelings are intermingled— disgust for the evil which is gnawing at society, homesickness for the ideal, despair and hope, pessimism and optimism. Then as now, and as always, two cities, two "generations," coexist and confront one another—one is seeking God;[10] the other forgets him. Two "ways" (1:6; 16:4-9) call for man's choice. The Psalms describe in a wealth of detail the grimaces and gestures

[10]Pss. 13:6; 23:6; 72:15.

of the wicked man, his enterprises, his ways of acting, and his goals. Evil has many faces. It is the enemy,[11] the adversary,[12] the aggressor (58:2), the warrior,[13] the proud,[14] the violent,[15] the evildoer,[16] the mighty man (58:4), the fool (52:2; cf. 13:1), the champion of infamy (51:3), the sinner,[17] the man of blood (54:24; 58:3), of deceit (54:24), the man of wicked tongue (139:12), the evil man (139:2), the liar (57:4), the traitor (58:6), the devourer of men (56:5).

In short, evil is the flesh (55:5)—what is mortal (55:2), or simply man himself (55:12). The mystery of iniquity lies in the depths of the sons of Adam: "The scheme they have devised; deep are the thoughts of each heart" (63:7). In these souls sin swarms, but the just cause will gain the victory. "It will be proclaimed: truly there is a reward for the just; truly there is a God who is judge on earth!" (57:12.) "Men may know that God is the ruler of Jacob, yes, to the ends of the earth" (58:14).

Applications and Rereadings. Israel lived through many sombre hours of anguish, infidelity, and even apostasy. And yet, these Psalms ordinarily are assigned either to the postexilic era, or to the time of the Bab-

[11]Pss. 53:9; 54:4; 55:10; 58:2; 63:2.
[12]Pss. 53:7; 55:3; 58:11.
[13]Pss. 54:22; 55:3; 139:3.
[14]Pss. 53:5; 139:6.
[15]Pss. 53:5; 139:2, 3, 9, 12.
[16]Pss. 58:3; 63:3; 140:4, 9.
[17]Pss. 54:4; 57:4, 11; 139:9; 140:10.

ylonian occupation when victorious pagans led the vanquished astray (55:8; 58:6,9). The fool, the proud man, the devourer of the people, is identified with the godless foreigner who does not call upon God. Then he was master in the Holy Land where he recruited accomplices. Thus, a new class of enemies enters the scene: invaders, supported by false brothers, who are traitors to the faith (58:6). Christians recite these Psalms thinking of the persecutions foretold by the Lord: "The world will hate you . . . they will persecute you . . . they will kill you.[18] The Apostolic preaching orients us toward a Christian advancement. It does not turn us away from the royal road of the literal sense: "Our wrestling is not against flesh and blood, but against the Principality and the Powers, against the world-rulers of this darkness, against the spiritual forces of wickedness on high" (Eph. 6:12); "Your adversary, the devil, as a roaring lion, goes about seeking someone to devour. Resist him, steadfast in the faith" (1 Pt. 5:9).

In spite of the proliferation of sin and the assaults of evil forces, the Christian does not sink into pessimism but, with a conqueror's soul, takes up the good fight (Jn. 16:33; Rom. 8:31-39).

Moral disintegration is the worst of catastrophes for society. However, other disasters such as natural calamities, military defeats, and the loss of independence, at

[18]Jn. 15:18-16, 4; Mt. 5:11-12; 1 Pt. 4:12-16; 2 Tm. 3:12; Acts 5:41.

times hobble the life of an entire nation. In these circumstances, Israel reacts as did the sick man, the accused, or the exile, with individual supplications. His first movement thrusts him toward God the Savior (3 Kgs. 8:33 ff.). He multiplies his acts of penitence, offers sacrifice, and sings songs of lamentation.[19] Some prayers, which to begin with expressed individual stress, are re-employed to represent the feelings of the afflicted community. A short addition, often as a finale, amplifies the voice of the one praying and gives the Psalm a new dimension and a new weight of meaning: "Redeem Israel, O God, from all its distress!" (24:22.) "Save your people, and bless your inheritance; feed them, and carry them forever!" (27:9.) "Be bountiful, O Lord, to Sion in your kindness by rebuilding the walls of Jerusalem" (50:20). "Oh, that out of Sion would come the salvation of Israel! When God restores the well-being of his people, then shall Jacob exalt and Israel be glad" (52:7; 13:7).

It sometimes happens that an addition is used for a long supplication. Psalms 21, 68, 70, 89, and 101 are characteristic examples. This method of adaptation and updating consisted of adding glosses, amplifying the text, or placing texts side by side without carefully joining them. This is disconcerting to some exegetes who are overly inclined to sense incoherences and contradictions. The coexistence of individual and col-

[19]Jer. 36:9; 41:4 f.; Jl. 1:13; 2:13 ff.; 2 Sm. 24:21 ff.; 2 Par. 20.

lective details in the same poem also feeds the controversy between the individualistic and national interpretations of the Psalms.

In reality, the greater number of individual laments, even without addition and without correction, lend themselves to community use simply because of the analogy of the situations and the sentiments, but particularly by reason of Israel's personification. The nation was not considered an abstraction, but a living being who was born, grew up in the midst of difficulties, fell ill as a result of sin, grew old, stumbled, and got up again. "Much have they oppressed me from my youth; yet they have not prevailed against me. Upon my back the plowers plowed; long did they make their furrows. But the just Lord has severed the cords of the wicked" (128:2-4).[20] Some prayers seem to be individual, but are more probably the supplications of the community (76, 122).

COLLECTIVE SUPPLICATIONS

Various Calamities. The Psalter contains laments that are clearly collective.[21] Psalm 79 associated with the disaster in the realm of Samaria. Three of them (43, 73, 78) make allusions to the destruction of the holy city and to the day of Jerusalem (136:7). Still others refer to reverses following the Exile (59, 84). All could have been used on occasions of different types of public calamity. The problem of chronology

[20]Pss. 128:4; cf. 117:10-18; 130:2-3; Os. 5:13; 6:1-2; 11:1 ff.; 13:14; 14:6; Is. 1:5-6; Lam. 2:13; Dt., Is., *passim.*
[21]Pss. 43, 59, 73, 78, 79, 82, 84; cf. Lam. 5.

does not affect their essential meaning. These prayers, built with the same structure as individual lamentations, are ordinarily comprised of an invocation, a presentation of the situation, a call for help, the certainty of final salvation, and the beginnings of a thanksgiving. The prophetic description of the misfortunes of the nation occupies a large place. Israel is likened to a vine pillaged by casual travelers, ravaged by the wild boar of the woods, or by the beasts of the field (79:13-14). Military defeats are deplored: "You go not forth with our armies. You have let us be driven back by our foes" (43:10-11); "You have rejected us and broken our defenses . . . you have rocked the country and split it open . . . you have made your people feel hardships, you have raised for those who fear you a banner to which they may flee out of . . . . Have not you, O God, rejected us, so that you go not forth, O God, with our armies?" (59:3-6, 12.)

Here is a lamentable sight. The invasion and sacking of the country, the profanation of the sanctuary, and the massacre of those who dwell in the land: "You marked us out as sheep to be slaughtered . . . you sold your people for no great price; you made no profit from the sale of them" (43:12-13).

Jerusalem is nothing but a heap of ruins: "They have given the corpses of your servants as food to the birds of heaven, the flesh of your faithful ones to the beasts of the earth. They have poured out their blood like water round about Jerusalem, and there is no one to bury them" (78:2-3). The unhappy survivors are fed on the bread of tears and slake their thirst on their tears (79:6). The victorious enemy makes merry at the misfortune of the vanquished: "You made us the reproach of our neighbors, the mockery and scorn of those around us. You made us a byword among the nation . . . we have become the reproach of our neighbors, the scorn and derision of those around us" (43:14-15; 78:4; 79:7).[22] The country, like someone suffering a severe illness, prostrate in the dust, face to the ground, calls for healing: "Repair the cracks" (59:4). One psalmist places emphasis on the sacking of the Temple: "The nations have come into your inheritance; they have defiled your holy temple" (78:1). "Turn your steps toward the utter ruins; toward all the damage the enemy has done in the sanctuary. Your foes war triumphantly in your shrine; they have set up their tokens of victory. They are like men coming up with axes to a clump of trees; and now with chisel and hammer they hack at all its paneling. They set your sanctuary on fire; the place where your name abides they have razed and profaned" (73:3-7). It was unthinkable that the Lord could remain unfeeling before the vandalism that touched upon his very honor.

Imploring. Pleading follows lamentation: "Awake! Why are you sleeping? Arise! Help!" These are the calls for prompt intervention by God. At times, there

[22]Pss. 43:14-15; 78:4; 79:7.

is a protestation of innocence: "All this has come upon us, though we have not forgotten you, nor have we been disloyal to your covenant" (43:18). Unlike the idolatrous nations, Israel never ceased to profess faith in one God. It was a people who prayed only to the true God (79:5).

Sometimes there was a confession of sin: "Remember not against us the iniquities of the past . . . pardon our sins" (78:8,9). The psalmist pleads the glorious memories of the past, the actions of God in nature, his great deeds in the nation's history[23] and, especially, the Covenant (73:20). In short, the honor of God and his love for Israel (43:4,27) were at stake (73:18; 78:10,12). The cause of the Chosen People is identified with that of God (59:3-4,13; 73:21). "We, your people and the sheep of your pasture, will give thanks to you forever; to all generations we shall declare your praise" (78:13). "O Lord of Hosts, restore us; if your face shine upon us, then we shall be saved" (79:20). At times, a comforting oracle stirs up the hope of the community at prayer (59:8-10).

The Trials of the Church. Near-Eastern literature has bequeathed us similar lamentations. Akkad, Ur, and Nippur underwent devastation and ruin as Jerusalem did. But our Psalms come forth victoriously from comparison with the Sumerian tablets recording

[23]Pss. 43:2 ff.; 59:10-12; 73:2, 12 ff.; cf. 21:5-6.

these sorrowful events.[24] There is no need to make a comparison by reciting collective supplications. It will be more profitable to reflect on the suffering of the Lord weeping over Jerusalem, on the spiritual setbacks more lamentable than temporal reverses, and on the scandals known to all Christian ages, and yet to be known through the passage of centuries.

[24]The texts referred to are unfortunately not available to many readers. They are treated in James B. Pritchard, editor, *Ancient Near Eastern Texts* (2nd edition; Princeton, New Jersey: Princeton University Press, 1955), pp. 455 ff.; and Adam Falkenstein and Wolfram von Soden, *Sumerische und Akkadische Hymnen und Gebete* (Zürich-Stuttgart: Artemis-Verlag, 1953), pp. 187 ff. Some fragments of these laments and briefer mention may be found in Samuel Noah Kramer, *History Begins at Sumer* (Doubleday Anchor Book; Garden City, New York: Doubleday & Company, Inc., 1959), pp. 226 ff.; and Henri and H. A. Frankfort, editors, *Before Philosophy* (Harmondsworth, Sussex: Penguin Books, 1954), pp. 154 ff.

[6]

From Supplication to Praise

Often in individual lamentations, the afflicted confessed their sins. Misfortune forced them to turn in upon themselves, to reflect, and so to recognize the evil that lies in the heart of man. They always proclaimed their trust, for there is no appeal without hope. But, because they were sure of being heard by their Lord, powerful, faithful, and compassionate, they thanked him. One or another of these three topics—consciousness of sin, trust in God, or thanksgiving—constitutes the exclusive, or at least predominant, theme of the prayers grouped in this chapter.

PSALMS OF PENITENCE

Penitential Formulae. Some of the unfortunate regarded their troubles as punishment for known or hidden sins. It was natural for them to seek to disarm the divine anger by confession. Confession draws pardon and grace obtains salvation: "Once I said, 'O Lord, have pity on me; heal me, though I have sinned against you'" (40:5).[1] Extrabiblical literature offers

[1]Cf. Pss. 6:2; 37:4-6, 19; 38:9; 39:13; 68:6.

us many examples of this type of supplication. These imperfect prayers—whose inspiration contains far too much calculation and self interest—are the witness to a still rudimentary theology.

The Psalter contains two supplications (50,129) that show more spiritual maturity; these figure to advantage among the penitential Psalms.[2]

The Sense of Sin. Psalm 50, the *Miserere*,[3] unique among the religious poems of mankind and jewel of the Psalter, moves us sinners to the very depths of our being. Here, there is no more talk of enemies, persecutors, or accusers. Instead, only one accuser occupies the stage, and he is the psalmist himself. Here, in spite of some possible allusions to a sickness (verse 6, punishment?; verse 9, leprosy?; verse 10, "crushed bones"; verse 16, death?), the suffering is no longer physical but repentant and draws forth lamentation. At last, the plea is raised to a level never to be surpassed. This man knew, as did his predecessors,

[2]Pss. 6, 31, 37, 50, 101, 139, 142; cf. the Psalm of Manasses in the appendix to the Vulgate.

[3]Cf. R. Galdos, "Psalmi 50, 'Miserere mei, Deus' exegetica explicatio," *Verbum Domini*, X (1930), 67-79; André Feuillet, "Le verset 7 du Miserere et le péché originel," *Recherches de Science Religieuse*, XXXII (1944), 5-26; J. Guillet, "Le Psaume Miserere," *La Maison-Dieu*, XXXIII (1953), 56-71; P. E. Bonnard, "Le Psaume de pénitence d'un disciple de Jérémie," *Bible et Vie chrétienne*, XVII (1957), 59-67; "Le vocabulaire du Miserere," *Mémorial Gelin, op. cit.*, pp. 145-56; E. Beaucamp, "Justice divine et pardon," *ibid.*, pp. 129-44.

that sin piles up many sorts of malice—fighting, revolt, perversity, and evil. All of these aspects are inlaid in the Hebrew words, but masked in their Latin translation: *peccatum, iniquitas, culpa, malum.*

But this author grasped far better than any of his predecessors the essential face of all evil, that is, offense against God: "For I acknowledge my offense, and my sin is before me always; Against you only have I sinned, and done what is evil in your sight" (5-6).

The psalmist so emphasizes this "theological" character that it is difficult to identify his sin concretely. Some exegetes employ elaborate reasoning to discover, for example, whether the sin represents an attack upon the rights of a neighbor, murder, or adultery (cf. v. 6). Others imagine different situations such as apostasy, joining in false worship, a crisis of despair, or skepticism. Such problems never crossed the minds of the ancients who ingenuously read the title: Psalm of David, when the prophet Nathan came to him after his sin with Bethsabee. To be sure, the great figure of David, sinner, penitent, at last at peace again with God, shows itself on the horizon. But we share the scruples of those exegetes who hesitate to attribute to him a composition that is so close to the preaching of Jeremiah, Ezechiel, and Second Isaiah in spirit and letter.

THE INBORN WEAKNESS OF MAN. Personal sin reveals the inherent weakness of man.[4] The psalmist,

---

[4]Cf. Pss. 57:4; 89:7 ff.; Gn. 8:21.

endowed with a keen sense of offense against God, throws a penetrating glance at his native condition: "Indeed, in guilt was I born, and in sin my mother conceived me." From his birth, even from conception, man is touched by sin. Sin comes with life itself. This is neither an excuse nor an attenuating circumstance intended to incline the Lord to indulgence. Instead, it is a second confession that justifies a more conscious and more pressing appeal to mercy and to the divine power. God alone can heal a being so deeply plunged into iniquity and restore rightness to his heart. The penitent, with moving insistence, calls in turn upon God's good will, his love, and motherly tenderness (v. 3; cf. Ex. 34:6).

EFFICACY OF THE DIVINE PARDON. Pardon is a gift. It is neither simple forgetfulness nor remission, but the effacing of revolt, the washing away of iniquity, and the cleansing of fault. "Wipe out my offense . . . thoroughly wash me from my guilt . . . cleanse me . . . cleanse me of sin with hyssop, that I may be purified . . . whiter than snow" (50:3-4,9). Pardon renews and causes a new birth, even a new creation (cf. 103:29-30):

A clean heart create for me, O God,
And a steadfast spirit renew within me . . .
Your holy spirit take not from me . . .
    and a willing spirit sustain in me. (50:12-14)

The intervention of God touches the very depths of being. It stirs up a new personality with a heart that is pure, stable, fervent, and freed by the spirit (cf. Ez. 36:25-27). Salvation drives out all sadness: "Let me hear the sounds of joy and gladness; the bones you have crushed shall rejoice . . . give me back the joy of your salvation" (50:10,14). Already, there is a thanksgiving and an odd sort of gratitude. Here, there are no enemies to be confounded or destroyed, only wanderers to be led back onto the right path. Pardon awakes an apostle's calling: "I will teach transgressors your ways, and sinners shall return to you" (50:15). Here, there are no animals immolated in sacrifice, but an inspired praise, the offering of a broken heart and spirit:

> O Lord, Open my lips,
>   and my mouth shall proclaim your praise.
> For you are not pleased with sacrifices;
>   should I offer a holocaust, you would not accept it.
> My sacrifice, O God, is a contrite spirit;
>   a heart contrite and humbled, O God, you will not
>   spurn. (50:17-19)

This prayer, however personal its accents (vv. 8, 12), is still written within the framework of the community. The psalmist feels himself in communion with a guilty nation, a faithless people, but one that is also, from its mother's womb,[5] broken by exile, repentant, witness of the "justice" of God (16:6), and so assured by the divine mercy of a material and spiritual restoration (30:20-21).

De Profundis! The Certainty of Pardon. The author of Psalm 129 appears less obsessed with his own

---

[5]Is. 48:8; Ez. 16:44-45; 19:1-2, 10.

wretchedness, and more attracted by God's mercy.[6] He does not linger over the picture of his sorry state. One sole image, the symbol of his great distress, is enough for his purpose. Sin is a gulf. Out of this abyss, out of the depths, his call for help rises: "I cry . . . I trust . . . I wait . . ." (1,5,6). This is a discreet and indirect confession; the psalmist is a sinner lost in a sinful mass:

If you, O Lord, mark iniquities,
Lord, who can stand? (v. 3)

This implicit confession, picked out soberly in both light and shade, with shame and delicacy, renders above all homage to God's immeasurable goodness. The Lord disposes of an inexhaustible treasure of grace, pardon, and redemption:

But with you is forgiveness . . . .
For with the Lord is kindness,
    and with him is plenteous redemption. (vv. 4, 7)

Clemency does not encourage cowardice; it calls to God's service, fosters filial fear, joy, and hope. Pardon appears to the psalmist and his people—always against this background of the community—as surely as the dawn appears after the night: "My soul waits for the Lord more than sentinels wait for the dawn. More than sentinels wait for the dawn, let Israel wait for the Lord" (vv. 6-7).

[6]R. Arconada, "Psalmus 129 (130), 'De profundis' retentus, emendatus, glossatus," *Verbum Domini*, XII (1932), 213-19.

These two Psalms permeate Christian piety. The
De profundis, associated with the liturgy for the dead,
sometimes instills sadness. Its joyous tonality should
be restored for the cheerfulness that suits the redeemed. As for the *Miserere,* it flowers often in the
liturgy: the *Incipit* of Matins; song of the *Asperges*
before the High Mass on Sunday; reminiscenses in
the *Kyrie Eleison* and, perhaps, in the *Veni Creator.*
Above all, this Psalm has given essential meaning to
the term "contrition," to the vocabulary and theology
of penance. Its author had learned the profound meaning of moral evil by listening in the intimacy of his
heart to the lesson of the teacher of wisdom (v. 8).
The cross shows Christians the gravity of sin, the
extent and richness of grace, and the value of inner
sacrifice, but especially the extraordinary love of God
for men. God so loved the world; mercy continues and
even goes far beyond that of the Psalm.

PRAYERS OF TRUST

The feeling of trust prevails in a number of Psalms.[7]
On the one hand, the call to help, the presentation of
the psalmist's case, and the lament disappear or are
much reduced. Trust, on the other hand, the main-
spring of every prayer, comes into the foreground.
These prayers with a lofty religious bearing emanate,
it seems, from Levitical circles.[8] There is no need to
suppose the existence of a special brotherhood of "spir-

[7] Pss. 4, 10, 15, 22; 26:1-6; 61, 90, 120, 124, 130.
[8] Pss. 4, 10, 15, 22, 26; cf. Pss. 41, 42, 62.

ituals" in the shadow of the Temple. These psalmists sing their security in peace and joy, perhaps on the occasion of a sacrifice of thanksgiving. They sing it ordinarily as a profession of faith and invite their fellow citizens to share their experience.

Security in Peace and Joy. Variations on this theme of security are reckoned among the most beautiful passages of the Psalter. There is the security of the pampered lamb, led and guarded by the divine Shepherd:[9] "Even though I walk in the dark valley, I fear no evil; for you are at my side with your rod and your staff that give me courage" (22:4). The same thought is expressed with more warlike images, in Psalm 26:[10] "The Lord is my light, my salvation; whom should I fear? The Lord is my life's refuge; of whom should I be afraid? Though an army encamp against me, my heart will not fear; though war be waged upon me, even then will I trust" (26:1, 3; cf. 3:7). Here, finally, is the more tender scene of a babe nestling on his mother's lap: "Nay rather, I have stilled and quieted my soul like a weaned child. Like a weaned child on its mother's lap [so is my soul within me]" (130:1-2). Another gives us a detail to be relished because his abandonment to God frees him from sleeplessness: "As soon as I lie down, I fall peacefully asleep, for

[9]Cf. E. Vogt, "The 'Place in Life' of Ps. 23," *Biblica*, XXXIV (1953); E. Beaucamp, "Vers les pâturages de Yahvé, Ps. 23 (22)," *Bible et Vie chrétienne*, XXXII (1960), 47-57.

[10]A. Rose, "Le Seigneur est ma lumière, Ps. 27 (26)," *Bible et Vie chrétienne*, XXIII (1958), 70-82.

you alone, O Lord, bring security to my dwelling" (4:9; cf. 3:6). This picturesque remark predestined Psalm 4 to become a night prayer. In the background of Psalm 10, social troubles inviting attack by the wicked may be divined. Some prudent people count on the just man to take to the hills; but the man who is righteous of heart reacts vigorously. He will never flee to the mountains. There is but one refuge, the Lord. "In the Lord I take refuge; how can you say to me, flee to the mountain like a bird?" (10:1.)

Permanent Intimacy with God. The text, whose fullness is revealed by the New Testament (Acts 2:25-28; 13:35), describes the present and future joy of the devout man who gives himself to God generously, enthusiastically, and irrevocably: "Therefore my heart is glad and my soul rejoices, my body, too, abides in confidence; because you will not abandon my soul to the nether world, nor will you suffer your faithful one to undergo corruption. You will show me the path to life, fullness of joys in your presence, the delights at your right hand forever" (15:9-11). Thanks to his intimacy with God, the "saint," dazzled with light, joy, and peace, aspires to a communion that defies death. In Jesus, the Saint par excellence, these presentiments of the Levite are given an incomparable reality.[11]

[11]A. Vaccari, "Psalmi 15 (Vulg.) interpretatis catholica," *Verbum Domini,* XIII (1933), 321-32; L. Jaquet, "Yahweh, mon bonheur, c'est toi!" *Bible et Vie chrétienne,* XLIII (1962), 27-41.

God Alone. The profession of faith, source of so much trust, is resumed in two words: *God alone.*

> I say to the Lord, "My Lord are you.
> Apart from you I have no good." . . .
> O Lord, my alloted portion and my cup,
>   you it is who hold fast my lot.
> For me the measuring lines have fallen on pleasant sites;
>   fair to me indeed is my inheritance.
> (15:2,5-6; cf. Nm. 18:20-24; Dt. 10:9; 18:2)

This absolute and exclusive attachment to the true God (a satisfaction reserved for the "saints," that is to say, to pious Jews), this intransigent attitude makes him impervious to compromise: "They multiply their sorrows who court other gods. Blood libations to them I will not pour out nor will I take their names upon my lips" (15:4). The Levite of Psalm 4 is devoted also to the sovereign good in spite of the evil example of his compatriots, men "heavy of heart," sensualists and skeptics, reduced by nothingness and lying (idolatry?). He preaches to them. The role of dialogue, admonition, and the didactic preoccupation in this type of poem should be noted in passing. For his part, the psalmist takes delight in the divine favor:

> You put gladness into my heart,
>   more than when grain and wine abound. (4:8)

Care for teaching is emphasized in Psalms 61 and 90. The first is a lyric commentary on the motto, "God alone," "You alone, O Lord" (4:9). The other is a lesson of abandonment illustrated with examples. Psalm 61 seems like an enchantment as the poet repeats and mulls over the same formulae. He exhorts himself, then breathes forth his conviction to others: "Only in God is my soul at rest . . . he only is my rock and my salvation, my stronghold . . . only in God be at rest, my soul . . . with God is my safety and my glory . . . power belongs to God, and yours, O Lord, is kindness."

And like the other side of a coin here is another description, the definition of man and his resources: "What is man? A sagging fence, a battered wall . . . a breath . . . less than a breath" (61:10; cf. 145:3-4). Their resources are hypocrisy, violence, rapine, and disappointing riches (vv. 5, 11). The conclusion is: "Trust in him at all times, O my people" (v. 9). As individuals, the theocratic nation rests upon God alone. Material forces, the prestige of leaders, treaties, all these are vanity. "It is better to take refuge in the Lord than to trust in man. It is better to take refuge in the Lord than to trust in princes" (117:8-9). "A king is not saved by a mighty army, nor is a warrior delivered by great strength. Useless is the horse for safety; great though its strength, it cannot provide escape" (32:16-17). "Some are strong in chariots; some in horses, but we are strong in the name of the Lord, our God" (19:8).[12]

Privileges of One Who Takes Refuge with God. And here, in conclusion, is the charter of the privileges

[12]Cf. Pss. 106:13; 124:1-2; 126:1-2; 146:10-11.

for one who takes refuge in God. Psalm 90, indeed, details the plan of defense that the Lord carries out in favor of the righteous man. Protection is offered against the dangers of death, the attacks of the enemy, and contagious diseases. Security is assured at every moment, night or day, at high noon, and in every circumstance against secret or declared enmities. God, the guardian, is always on the alert—"He neither slumbers nor sleeps, the guardian of Israel" (120:4) —defending his protegé in his person and his goods throughout the ordinary affairs of daily life. He does not hesitate to mobilize his angels as a counterforce against the devilish adversaries: "You shall not fear the terror of the night nor the arrow that flies by day; nor the pestilence that roams in the darkness, nor the devastating plague at noon . . . no evil shall befall you, nor shall affliction come near your tent, for to his angels he has given command about you, that they guard you in all your ways" (90:5-6; 10:11).

An oracle (90:14-16), the signature of God, sets the seal of authenticity on what is a kind of contract. God's promise answers man's engagement (90:2,14). This Psalm, sometimes considered as a fragment of a liturgy on entering the Temple (cf. Pss. 14;23) or of a ritual to obtain a cure, enjoyed a great popularity in time of war (cf. v. 7) or during an epidemic. It is recommended for night prayer, but as prayer not as a talisman.

The Christian broadens the perspective of the Psalm. To be the beneficiary of a long life (90:16), to lead a peaceable existence sheltered from the dangers which menace our well-being and our homes, is an appreciable favor. But the greatest of perils consists in wandering away from the service of God (Mt. 4:6; Lk. 4:10 ff.). The Psalms of trust contain a vocabulary that is easy to broaden, a terminology most apt for expressing our childlike surrender into God's hands. To take refuge in the Lord, to rest in him, to cleave to him, to contemplate his face, to see his salvation, to share in his table—all these acts take on, by the light of the theology of grace and of glory, an import unsuspected by the psalmist. Once more, we can place an added burden on the texts without altering them.

THANKSGIVINGS

Structure. If individual thanksgivings are relatively few,[13] it may be that this is because men forget to say thanks (Lk. 17:17-18). More likely, however, the hymns and the prayers of trust took the place of songs of gratitude. Thanksgiving was already outlined and foretold in the supplication.[14] In fact, pleas, trust, and thanks are but three psychological moments of a single spiritual experience. After having been heard, the sick man, the persecuted, the refugee, the innocent, or the sinner, goes up to the Temple, accompanied by his relatives and friends, to offer a sacrifice: "I will extol you, O Lord, for you drew me clear" (29:2); "I will bless the Lord at all times . . . he answered

[13]Pss. 29, 31, 33, 39, 91, 114-115, 137.
[14]Pss. 21:26; 55:13; 60:9.

me" (33:2,5); "I love the Lord because he has heard
my voice in supplication" (114:1); "I will give thanks
to you, O Lord, with all my heart, for you have heard
the words of my mouth" (137:1).

After this prelude, the counterpart of the invocation
in Psalms of distress, the psalmist tells the story of
his deliverance. This narration—a characteristic element—is laid out according to a very simple plan.
There is the recalling of the distress (sickness and sin,
danger of death, persecution, etc.), then the call for
help, and finally the answer.[15] Ordinarily, the faithful
soul who has been heard recalls his earlier misfortunes
(attacks, persecutions, sickness, and sin), in figurative
and pathetic terms: abysses, floods, the grave, the gates
of Sheol, nets, arrows, slippery ground. "The breakers
of death surged round about me, the destroying floods
overwhelmed me; the cords of the nether world en-
meshed me, the snares of death overtook me. In my
distress I called upon the Lord" (17:5-7; 114:3-4);
"As long as I would not speak, my bones wasted away
with my groaning all the day, for day and night your
hand was heavy upon me; my strength was dried up
as by the heat of summer . . . then I acknowledged
my sin to you" (31:3-5).

God reverses this situation: he delivers, lifts up,
brings back to life, draws up from Sheol, from the pit
and the mire, and from the great waters, "I cried out

[15]Cf. 1 Sm. 2:1-10; Jn. 2; Is. 38:10-20: the canticle of
Ezechia; Lk. 1:46-55, 68-79.

to you, and you healed me. O Lord, you brought me up from the nether world; you preserved me from among those going down into the pit" (29:3-4); "For he has freed my soul from death, my eyes from tears, my feet from stumbling. I shall walk before the Lord in the lands of the living" (114:8-9);[16] "He stooped toward me and heard my cry. He drew me out of the pit of destruction, out of the mud of the swamp; he set my feet upon a crag; he made firm my steps" (39:2-3). There is an even more spectacular description in the thanksgiving of the king (17:8-20; cf. 143:5-8). To give thanks, the faithful soul sings and sacrifices:

How shall I make a return to the Lord
  for all the good he has done for me?
The cup of salvation I will take up,
  and I will call upon the name of the Lord;
My vows to the Lord I will pay
  in the presence of all his people . . . .
To you will I offer sacrifice of thanksgiving,
  and I will call upon the name of the Lord . . .
  in the courts of the house of the Lord,
  in your midst, O Jerusalem.
(115:3-5, 8-10; cf. 65:13-15)

Song and Sacrifice. The Psalms are the frame in which sacrifice was set. These two elements of ritual

[16]Cf. L. Deiss, "Je marcherai en présence de Yahweh, Ps. 116 (114-115)," *Bible et Vie chrétienne,* XXXIX (1961), 37-53.

even bore the same name.[17] Thanksgiving naturally
tends to glorify God: "And he put a new song into my
mouth, a hymn to our God" (39:4). Hence, we have
the frequency of hymnic elements:[18] "Gracious is the
Lord and just; yes our God is merciful. The Lord
keeps the little ones; I was brought low and he saved
me" (114:5-6).

> For his anger lasts but a moment;
>   a lifetime, his good will.
> At nightfall, weeping enters in,
>   but with the dawn, rejoicing. (29:6)

The psalmist becomes preacher, witness, moralist,
and apostle.[19] It is more than probable that the clergy,
keepers of these *ex-voto* Psalms, accentuated their didactic aspect, with a view to edification and instruction.[20]

Ceremonies of Thanksgiving. Two Psalms (106;117)
merit special attention. The first is like a paraliturgy
where, under the direction of the master of ceremonies,
pass four privileged groups: members of a caravan
returned from the desert (4-9); freed captives (10-16);
sick men healed (17-22); and men rescued from the
sea (23-32). Couplets, identical in structure, each a
thanksgiving in miniature, make up a description, an

[17]Jn. 2:10; Ps. 49:14, 23; 106:22.
[18]Cf. Pss. 17, 33, 65, 106.
[19]Pss. 21:23 ff.; 39:10-12; 31:8 ff.
[20]Cf. 31:1-2, 6 ff.; 33: an alphabetic Psalm that smells
of the lamp and the writer's trade, 39:5; 40:2-4.

invitatory, and a refrain. Here is the strophe consecrated to those who go down to the sea in ships:

They who sailed the sea in ships,
  trading on the deep waters,
  these saw the works of the Lord
  and his wonders in the abyss.
His command raised up a storm wind
  which tossed its waves on high.

They mounted up to heaven; they sank to the depths;
  their hearts melted away in their plight.
They reeled and staggered like drunken men,
  and all their skill was swallowed up.
They cried to the Lord in their distress . . .
He hushed the storm to a gentle breeze,
  and the billows of the sea were stilled;
  they rejoiced . . .
Let them give thanks to the Lord for his kindness.
(106:23-31)

The pulse of the liturgy may be even more easily demonstrated in Psalm 117, the song of the resurrection of Israel. There is a dialogue of entry (cf. 23:7-10; 14; 90), then chorus and response, procession, drawing up of the cortege about the altar, and finally the priestly blessing. We can picture the different actors (priests, Levites, laymen, leader), their gestures (117:27), and their songs. Israel, encircled by enemies who plan her fall (117:13) and death (cf. 65:9), gains a victory with God's help. In this, the suffering resurrection of Jesus prefigured.

All the nations encompassed me;
   in the name of the Lord I crushed them . . .
I was hard pressed and was falling,
   but the Lord helped me . . . .

The right hand of the Lord has struck with power:
   the right hand of the Lord is exalted;
   the right hand of the Lord has struck with power.

I shall not die, but live . . .
   though the Lord has indeed chastised me,
   yet he has not delivered me to death.

Open to me the gates of justice;
   I will enter them and give thanks to the Lord.
This gate is the Lord's; the just shall enter it.
(117:10, 13, 15-20)

Then the leader gives thanks, alternating his prayer
with the choir, the crowd, and the priests. Israel, in
the course of its history, obtained many favors of restoration—"for the mercy of God endures forever." One
of the most striking of these was the return from
Exile:

Had not the Lord been with us,
   let Israel say,
   had not the Lord been with us—
when men rose up against us,
   then would they have swallowed us alive.
When their fury was inflamed against us,
   then would the waters have overwhelmed us;
   the torrent would have swept over us;
   over us then would have swept
   the raging waters.

Blessed be the Lord, who did not leave us
   a prey to their teeth.
We were rescued like a bird
   from a fowler's snare;
   broken was the snare,
   and we were freed. (123:1-8)

The same accents may be discerned in another
Psalm of resurrection (65), but the thanksgiving there
is more widely extended:

Bless our God, you peoples,
   loudly sound his praise;
   he has given life to our souls,
   and has not let our feet slip.
For you have tested us, O God!
You have tried us as silver is tried by fire;
   you have brought us into a snare;
   you have laid a heavy burden on our backs.
You let men ride over our heads;
   we went through fire and water,
   but you have led us out to refreshment. (65:8-12)

Then, one who prays, numbers his generous intentions in detail, not without some satisfaction:

I will bring holocausts to your house;
   to you I will fulfill the vows
   which my lips uttered
   and my words promised in my distress.
Holocausts of fatlings I will offer you.
With burned offerings of rams;
   I will sacrifice oxen and goats. (65:13-15)

A people who have been saved speaks as one person. Hence, the ease with which individual thanks-

givings are transformed into collective prayers (cf. the titles of Psalms 29; 39; 137). In the supplications, the certainty of being heard tempered sorrow, for joy was mixed with the tears. An analogous phenomenon is produced in the thanksgiving. The confident plea is joined to thanks, for fears of the future cast their shadow on the cheerfulness of the present. Let the Lord complete his work! To call forth new favors is to give thanks for old ones.

> You have favored, O Lord, your land;
>> you have restored the well-being of Jacob.
> You have forgiven the guilt of your people;
>> you have covered all their sins.

> Restore us, O God our Savior,
>> and abandon your displeasure against us . . .
> Show us, O Lord, your kindness,
>> and grant us your salvation . . . . (84:2-3,5,8)

> The Lord has done great things for us;
>> we are glad indeed.
> Restore our fortunes, O Lord,
>> like the torrents in the southern desert.
> Those that sow in tears
>> shall reap rejoicing.
> Although they go forth weeping,
>> carrying the seed to be sown,
>> they shall come back rejoicing.
>> carrying their sheaves. (125:3-6)

> The Lord will complete what he has done for me;
>> your kindness, O Lord, endures forever;
>> forsake not the work of your hands. (137:8)

The Psalm of thanksgiving then appears as a very rich type. It is related to supplications, to prayers of trust, and to hymns. In addition to this, it contains wisdom and didactic elements. Better than all this, the Jewish thanksgiving of song and sacrifice, memorial of suffering, expression of well-being in deliverance, and the public proclamation of faith and trust, foretells *sacrum convivium . . . recolitur memoria passionis . . . mens impletur gratia . . . futurae gloriae pignus*—the Eucharist:—"sacred banquet . . . recalling the memory of His passion . . . filling the mind with grace . . . and giving the pledge of future glory."

⟦7⟧

Sit Thou at My Right Hand

A number of Psalms, focused on the person of the king, make up a special, although not entirely homogeneous, family. This type is at times close to that of supplication, at others to thanksgiving, and, at still others, to prophetic oracles. Whether appropriate to this or that circumstance, these songs offer a rich variety of structure, style, and theme. It is impossible to fit them all into an identical picture. Their unity comes from their original circle, the court; and from the person they treat, the king. In the religious life of Israel, four privileged classes of men exercised a preponderant influence. They were priests, prophets, wise men, and kings. Modern exegesis recognizes and underlines the characteristic traits of the royal function in antiquity. In spite of exaggerations, even extravagences—for in the enthusiasm of discoveries, one easily succumbs to the attraction of a systematic explanation —some historians freely admit the existence of a theology of the kingship, an ideology widespread in the ancient world. It is important to read the Psalms in this special light.

Kings of Nations and the King of Jerusalem

Egypt likened its pharaoh to a god. He was the incarnation of Horus. The Mesopotamians, without deifying their monarch, nonetheless raised him to the sphere of the divine. As high priest of the city, the king played an eminent role in the liturgy. Of him a conventional, hieratic language was used. The style of the court blossomed with pompous and hyperbolic phraseology. From the time of Solomon on, the palace on Mt. Sion was inspired by Egyptian protocol. Formulae of etiquette employed at Ras Shamrah, Assyria, and in Babylonia can be identified, more or less clearly, in the praises in honor of the king of Jerusalem. But Israel was faithful to her own particular style, history, and faith. Before incorporating them into her own living tradition, she sifted, rectified, and assimilated these practices. Among other peoples, the origin of kingship coincided with the nations' beginnings. At Ras Shamrah, as well as in Egypt and Mesopotamia, the notion of monarchy was deeply rooted in primitive soil. It was both mythological and naturistic.

There was nothing of the sort in Israel. That kingdom began its history at a relatively late date (1020 B.C.). Accordingly, as a kingdom, it was regarded as an upstart and encountered lively opposition. The world into which it was brought had, for a long time, been swayed by different influences and reacted accordingly. Israel—this come-lately institution—had to take into account social and religious traditions of long standing, as well as the presence of an installed clergy, in order to carve itself a place. That is why the ideology of royalty passing through Israel left its influence, but was transformed to bring it into agreement with the monotheistic faith. It was adapted, then, to the manners and customs of an already well-organized people.

THE PROPHECY OF NATHAN

A singular fact marked the countenance of the Israelite monarchy and left a permanent impression. This was the oracle given to David by Nathan: "And when your days are finished, and you are laid with your fathers, I will raise up your heir after you, who shall be born of your bodies; and I will establish his kingdom. He shall build a house for my name, and I will establish the throne of his kingdom forever. I will be a father to him, and he shall be a son to me. . . . Your house and your kingdom shall be confirmed before me forever; your throne shall be established forever" (2 Sm. 7:12-16). It was this oracle, renewed and commented on by the prophets, that brought about the elaboration of a truly original concept of kingship in Israel. The prophecy of Nathan, "the backbone of later Jewish history," "the pivot and axis of salvation," begins a decisive phase in that history. The hopes attached to the seed of the woman (Gn. 3:15), the Covenant contracted with Abraham (Gn. 12:2-3), renewed with the patriarchs (Gn. 26:2-5, 24; 28:13-18), and made more precise in relationship to Judah (Gn. 49:8-12) and Israel (Nm. 24), were now to be concentrated on a single man, the king. God entered into an agreement with David and his House (2 Sm. 23:5; Is. 55:3). From that time on, the dynasty ful- filled the Covenant and produced the heir of the old promises.

The King, Chosen of God. Israel was the object of God's choice and its king would enjoy the same favor.

I myself have set up my king
    on Sion, my holy mountain . . . (2:6)

I have made a covenant with my chosen one,
    I have sworn to David my servant . . . (88:4)
The Lord swore to David
    a firm promise from which he will not withdraw:
    "Your own offspring I will set upon your throne."
(131:11-12)

Adopted Son of Yahweh. The Lord treated Israel as his child (Ex. 4:22). The king, on the day of his enthronement, was granted the same privilege: "I will proclaim the decree of the Lord, the Lord said to me, 'You are my Son; this day I have begotten you'" (2:7). That idea, briefly developed, is seen in an archaic piece in honor of David. The mythological reminis- cences are not offensive to monotheistic orthodoxy: "Yours is princely power in the day of your birth, in holy splendor; before the daystar, like the dew, I have begotten you" (109:3). The exact measure of these bold affirmations must be viewed in the light of Na- than's prophecy. Adoption introduced the monarch into the divine intimacy. A court poet would force the hyperbole to its extreme limit: "Your throne, O God, stands forever and ever" (44:7).

Mediator. Israel, consecrated to God, formed a kingdom of priests (Ex. 19:6). A priestly mediation was incumbent on the king as well. Psalm 109 explicitly grants David the title of priest: "The Lord has sworn, and he will not repent: 'You are a priest forever, according to the order of Melchisedec'" (109:4). David, like the king of Salem (Gn. 14:18), had to bear the burdens of a chief, both political and religious. The ancient kings performed the acts for which the priesthood would later claim monopoly, but they did not raise themselves to the level of the high priesthood.

The prince, a religious personage, stands on a different level from that of the priests. He did not enter into the priestly hierarchy but stood over it. However, he was interposed as the mediator between God and the people. Thanks to him and through him, divine blessings descended on the nation which he embodied. The successes or failures of the kingdom, the prosperity or desolation of the country depended on his conduct, good or evil. His subjects owed him the very breath in their nostrils (Lam. 4:20). He was the lamp of Israel (2 Sm. 21:17).

Messiah. In sum, the duties, rights, and beneficence of the king were derived from the fact that he was the Anointed of the Lord.[1] He who sits on the throne

[1] Pss. 2:2; 131:10; cf. 27:8; 83:10.

of David—throne of God[2]—becomes, by his consecration, an anointed one—a Christ—holy and inviolable. With the foundation of the dynasty, Messianism took wing. To be sure, the expectation of salvation did not commence with David. But, beginning with the hereditary kingship, the hope of a Savior was embodied in a royal personage. This hope will be made more precise, further developed, and refined by the oracles of the prophets.[3]

ROYAL POEMS

At least ten royal poems can be counted.[4] Other royal prayers may have lost their primitive character because of their frequent use by the common people. But one must renounce the idea of restoring the breviary of the prince because the leader used the same literary forms as his subjects (supplication, prayer, and thanksgiving). It is also suspected that some poets may have composed verses on the model of the royal poems for individuals or the community as a whole (143).

Songs of Consecration. Some songs are related, it seems, to the liturgy of enthronement. Among others

---

[2]Pss. 109:1; cf. 1 Par. 28:5; 29:23; 2 Par. 9:8.

[3]Am. 9:11 ff.; Os. 3:5; Is. 7:9 ff.; 11:1 ff.; Mi. 2:12-13; 5:1 ff.; Jer. 17:25; 23:1-6; 30:8; 33:17 ff.; Ez. 34:23 ff.; 37:24; Za. 9:9-10.

[4]Pss. 2, 17, 19, 20, 44, 71, 88, 100, 109, 131.

is the *Dixit Dominus*[5] that breaks forth with a flourish at the beginning of Vespers for Sunday: "The Lord said to my Lord: 'Sit at my right hand, till I make your enemies your footstool'" (109:1). The handing over of the scepter, instrument of power (2:9), and symbol of the judges' office (44:7), signified the transmission of powers to God's delegate, his adopted son. This virtually established the king as the head of the people (2:8-12; 17:44 ff.; 88:28). "The scepter of your power the Lord will stretch forth from Sion: 'Rule in the midst of your enemies'" (109:2).

Some exegetes suspect, in the finale of the Psalm, an allusion to the rite of washing at the fountain of Gihon, the sacred spring of Jerusalem (cf. 3 Kgs. 1:33, 38, 45): "From the brook by the wayside he will drink; therefore will he lift up his head" (109:7). Psalm 2 may also figure in the Book of Consecration. It recalls the themes and the phases of the ceremony: anointing (v. 6); Covenant with David, divine sonship (v. 7); promises of victory, and the homage of his subjects (vv. 8 ff.). Psalm 100, a type of "discourse from the throne" or "mirror of kings," was doubtless pronounced in similar circumstances.

[5]Evode Beaucamp, "Au roi de Sion, Ps. 110 (109)," *Bible et Vie chrétienne*, XLII (1962), 32-49; Raymond Tournay, "Le Psaume CX," *Revue Biblique*, LXVII (1960), sums up what is essential on kingship in Israel, 5-41. Roland de Vaux, *Ancient Israel*, trans. John McHugh (New York: McGraw-Hill Book Company, 1961), pp. 100 ff.; cf. also J. De Fraine, *L'aspect religieux de la royauté, israélite* (Rome: Pontificio Instituto Biblica, 1954).

Prayer for the Leader of the Armies. The trials of political life furnished many occasions for national prayers. Before the departure for war, intercession was made for the chief of the armies (Ezechia?):

The Lord answer you in time of distress;
    the name of the God of Jacob defend you!
May he send you help from the sanctuary,
    from Sion may he sustain you.
May he remember all your offerings,
    and graciously accept your holocaust.
May he grant you what is in your heart
    and fulfill your every plan.
May we shout for joy at your victory
    and raise the standards in the name of our God.

O Lord, grant victory to the king,
    and answer us when we call upon you. (19:2-6,10)

Te Deum! On the return of victorious troops, the king (17) or the community (20), intoned the *Te Deum* of thanksgiving (cf. Ex. 15; Jgs. 5). This latter Psalm would fit equally well a ceremony of crowning or the anniversary of the king's consecration (of Ezechia?). The mention of the crown supports this hypothesis: "For you welcomed him with goodly blessings, you placed on his head a crown of pure gold. He asked life of you: You gave him length of days forever and ever" (20:4-5).[6]

[6]Evode Beaucamp, "Tu le combles de joie, Ps. 21 (20)," *Bible et Vie chrétienne,* XXII (1958), 78-88.

Bridal Song. Everything concerned with the person of the prince takes on a religious character. Psalm 44—a song of love, according to the title, a marvel of literature to poets, but a riddle to many commentators—glorifies a royal couple (Achab and Jezabel?). The bridal song sketches the portrait of an ideal king, possessing unique beauty, greater than that of man, the result of divine blessing: "Fairer in beauty are you than the sons of men; grace is poured out upon your lips; thus God has blessed you forever" (v. 3). The hero, (v. 4; cf. Is. 9:5), girds on his sword—his glory and his honor—prepared to do combat for the most noble causes of faith and righteousness. His right hand does these mighty deeds. From his chariot, he aims his sharp arrows at his disheartened enemies. He brings the people under his yoke (cf. 2:9; 17:38-43; 20:9 ff.).

His policy within the kingdom shines with equal brilliance. It is natural for the king, a divine being, to govern with righteousness and justice. His throne is in no danger of being overthrown by revolt: "Your throne, O God, stands forever and ever; a tempered rod is your royal scepter. You love justice and hate wickedness; therefore God, your God, has anointed you with oil of gladness above your fellow kings" (44:7-8). And the poet, whose heart is bubbling over with inspiration (v. 2), lists the outward signs of the royal happiness—the splendor of his garments, the richness of his palace, and the pleasant music of the lutes. The call by her husband demands a sacrifice of his bride. She must forget her own people, even her family, to respond only to the king's love, her lord. The warning, a quiet reminder of the first marriage (Gn. 2:24), is accompanied by an alluring reward: "And the city of Tyre is here with gifts; the rich among the people seek your favor" (v. 13). The entrance into the palace provides for a description in iridescent colors: "All glorious is the king's daughter as she enters; her raiment is threaded with spun gold. In embroidered apparel she is borne in to the king; behind her the virgins of her train are brought to you. They are borne in with gladness and with joy; they enter the palace of the king" (44:14-16). And, the poet concludes, as is fitting, there are the good wishes that princes born of this union will carry on the famous line.[7]

In Trial. Like all men, kings know not only favorable days. One Psalm (88) is intermingled with hymnal couplets (2:3; 6:19), reminiscenses of an oracle (4:5; 20:38), and prophetic lamentations (39-52). It describes the unhappy lot of the descendant of David (Sedecia?). Here is a sharp contrast to the promises of yesteryear: "Yet you have rejected and spurned and been enraged at your anointed. You have renounced the covenant with your servant, and defiled his crown in the dust. You have broken down all his walls; you

[7]Evode Beaucamp, "Le'Oint de Yahweh et la Princesse éstrangère, Ps., 45 (44)," *Bible et Vie Chrétienne*, XXVIII (1959), 34-45.

have laid his strongholds in ruins. All who pass by the
way have plundered him; he is made the reproach of
his neighbors. You have exalted the right hands of his
foes, you have gladdened all his enemies. You have
turned back his sharp sword and have not sustained
him in battle. You have deprived him of his luster
and hurled his throne to the ground. You have short-
ened the days of his youth; you have covered him
with shame" (vv. 39-46).

The Ideal King. Reverses tear and rend illusions,
but they can also spur hope. God does not wish to
annihilate but to cleanse. Trial opens the eyes. The
day came when Israel dreamt of the King of the future
who would succeed where his predecessors failed lam-
entably. Prayer is offered for his coming; an ideal
picture of him is drawn: "O God, with your judgment endow the king, and with your justice the king's
son; he shall govern your people with justice and your
afflicted ones with judgment. He shall defend the
afflicted among the people, save the children of the
poor, and crush the oppressor . . ." (71:1-2,4).

This king, true spiritual son of the prophet,[8] patterns
his conduct on the divine government (35:7; 88:15;
96:2). He wins fertility, well-being, and peace for
his country and his subjects. "He shall be like rain
coming down on the meadow, like showers watering
the earth. Justice shall flower in his days, and pro-

[8] Is. 9:6; 11:4-5; 32:1; Jer. 23:5; 33:15.

found peace, till the moon be no more. May there be an abundance of grain upon the earth; on the tops of the mountains the crops shall rustle like Lebanon; the city dwellers shall flourish like the verdure of the fields" (71:6-7, 16).[9] His kingdom will be worldwide: "May he rule from sea to sea, and from the River [Euphrates] to the ends of the earth" (v. 8). As the second Isaiah[10] foretold, the most distant princes would give him a nearly divine homage: "The kings of Tharsis and the Isles shall offer gifts; the kings of Arabia and Saba shall bring tribute. All kings shall pay him homage, all nations shall serve him" (vv. 10-11; cf. 2:8; 88:26,28; Gn. 49:10). "There shall be no noise of battle nor clash of arms" (cf. 2:9; 109:5-6). "Yet this will be no military dictatorship, but the defense of the poor, the oppressed, and a blessing for all the tribes of the earth" (v. 17).[11]

CHRIST THE KING

The message of the angel Gabriel to the Virgin Mary echoes the prophecy of Nathan, fully orchestrated in the royal Psalms: "Your Son . . . will be great and will be called the Son of the Most High; and the Lord God will give him the throne of David, his

[9]Cf. Am. 9:13; Os. 2:23-24; Is. 41:18-19; 55:12-13; Ez. 34:26-27; 36:8-9; Zac. 8:12.

[10]Is. 43:3-4; 45:14; 49:7, 23; 60:6.

[11]Cf. Hilaire Duesberg, "La justice selon le coeur de Dieu, Ps. 72 (71)," *Bible et Vie chrétienne*, XLI (1961), 44-51; R. Pautrel, "Le style de cour et le Psaume LXXII," *Mémorial Gelin, op. cit.*, pp. 157-63.

father; he will rule over the house of Jacob forever; and of his kingdom there shall be no end" (Lk. 1:31-33). As always, reality surpasses expectations but—when given strength by a wonderful pre-established harmony —the poetic hyperboles, boldness of the court style, even mythological reminiscenses themselves, are peculiarly appropriate to the ineffable, Jesus. He who was consubstantial with the Father—eternal Priest, Savior, just, peaceful, and beneficent Prince—sovereign over all kings and lord of all people. There is no need to twist the texts to fit them to him. When the Christian event cast its brightness on the past with leaping flames, the true face of the King and the precise character of his reign is obvious.[12] Jesus calls God his father, but not as the kings of Jerusalem did. He *is* Priest and King, but more truly Priest than King, and a better one than Melchisedec and David. It is true that he wins striking victories, but he does not win them over dead bodies with a mace. He does not massacre, but converts, and gives life by his message and his sacrifice. The cross is his scepter; it is his servant and he is its master. The ideals of justice and peace that he proposes to the world are called the state of grace in Christian language. After transposition and transmutation by means of the fuller and typical senses, the royal Psalms are changed into prayers for the com-

[12]Cf. the articles "Roi" and "Messie," Xavier Léon-Dufoor, *et al.*, editors, *Vocabulaire de Théologie biblique* (Paris: Éditions du Cerf), cols. 942-949, 608-614.

ing of Christ the King, and then as now, into supplications in favor of political and religious leaders.

The Christian fact authorizes us to join texts which are apparently far apart and also to bring together lines which seem parallel. Since Jesus reigns in the world by his sacrifice, he fulfills at the same time the twofold prophetic figure of King and Suffering Servant. Thus, we have the right to join together the supplication of the just man afflicted and persecuted and the royal poems. They are heard together in the same symphony.

[[8]]

City of God

Jerusalem has striking titles heaped upon her. She is capital of the dynasty: "Set up judgment seats, seats for the house of David" (121:5). Jerusalem is the religious metropolis: "To it the tribes go up, the tribes of the Lord . . . to give thanks to the name of the Lord" (121:4). As heir to a prestigious past and destined for an exceptional future, Sion eclipsed the renown of Athens and Rome. Several Psalms[1] tell a litany of praises in her honor, sketch a mystique that idealizes the city: "His holy mountain, fairest of heights, joy of all the earth; 'recesses of the North,' is the city of the great King" (47:2-3). ". . . O city of God! . . . mother of peoples" (86:3-5) . . . "glory of Jacob" (46:5) . . . "dwelling of God" (75:3) . . . "perfect in beauty" (49:2).

DWELLING PLACE OF GOD

The origin of all these privileges is the choice of the Lord, made material by the transfer of the Ark to Jerusalem. The nomad sanctuary, closely associated with the changing fortunes of the people, symbolized

[1]Pss. 45, 47, 75, 83, 86, 121, 131, 132.

three centuries of trials and of wonders, from the epic of the desert to the entrance into the Holy Land, and the installation at Silo as the principal center of worship. There was much wandering and many tribulations before this rest in Sion. Psalm 131, sung perhaps at the annual commemoration of the twofold choice of the City and its King, embroiders the account of 2 Samuel, chapter seven: "Behold, we heard of it in Ephratha; we found it in the fields of Jaar. Let us enter into his dwelling, let us worship at his footstool" (131:6-7). As in the desert (Nm. 10:35), the signal for departure re-echoes: "Rise up, O Lord!" But, this time it is the final stage: "For the Lord has chosen Sion; he prefers her for his dwelling. Sion is my resting place forever; in her will I dwell. . . . In her will I make a horn to sprout forth for David; I will place a lamp for my anointed" (131:13-14, 17; cf. 78:68-69). A poet recounts in epic style a mosaic of recollections of ancient poems in the victorious cavalcade, or rather the solemn procession, of the Ark (cf. 67:2) to its final resting place.[2] From Sion, the Lord advances to the sanctuary, overlooking the rival, jealous mountains (67:17-19). This is the triumphant ascent of the Most High, the great King, in the midst of cheers and to the sound of trumpets:[3] "He brings people under us; nations under our feet. He chooses

---

[2]Raymond Tournay, "Le Psaume LXVII (67) et le Livre des Juges," *Revue Biblique*, LXVI (1959), 358-68.

[3]A. Caquot, "Le Psaume 47 (46) et la royauté de Yahwé," *Revue d'Histoire et de Philosophie religieuse*, XXXIX (1959), 311-17.

for us our inheritance, the glory of Jacob, whom he loves. God mounts his throne amidst shouts of joy" (46:4-6). Here is a liturgical echo of his taking possession of it:

> Lift up, O gates, your lintels;
>   reach up, you ancient portals,
>   that the king of glory may come in!
> Who is this king of glory?
> The Lord, strong and mighty,
>   the Lord, mighty in battle . . .
>   the Lord of hosts. (23:7-10)

The god of Israel finally supplants the local deity. The new capital, with its foundation upon the holy mountains (86:1), claims the title of "the recesses of the North," the name which Canaanite mythology gave to the dwelling place of the gods:

> Great is the Lord and wholly to be praised
>   in the city of our God.
> His holy mountains, fairest of heights,
>   is the joy of all the earth;
>   Mount Sion, "the recesses of the North,"
>   is the city of the great King. (47:2-3; cf. Is. 14:13)

In Jerusalem, corresponding to paradise, runs a river of joy and fertility, as once in Eden (Gn. 2:10):

> There is a stream whose runlets gladden the city of God,
>   the holy dwelling of the most high.
> (45:5; cf. Ez. 47:1-12; Ap. 22:1-2)

The abiding presence of the Almighty guarantees the stability and the security of the city. He inspires in the people an absolute trust amidst the most dramatic situations—cataclysms of nature, military catastrophes, earthquakes, the melting of the mountains, the boiling of the waters; the assaults of all leagues of enemies (45): "The Lord of hosts is with us; our stronghold is the God of Jacob" (45:8,12).

ISRAEL'S MEETING PLACE: SONGS OF ASCENT

Sion, the well beloved of God (86:2), became the joy and pride of Jacob (46:5). Pious Jews are on fire to climb the holy mountain.[4] One of them in his passionate fervor falls into a lover's rapture:

How lovely is your dwelling place,
   O Lord of Hosts!
My soul yearns and pines
   for the courts of the Lord.
My heart and my flesh
   cry out for the living God. (83:2-3; cf. 41:2-3)

The sanctuary is for men what a nest is for birds (83:4). The radiant happiness of Jerusalem's clergy and pilgrims is to be envied. "Happy they who dwell in your house! Continually they praise you. Happy the men whose strength you are! Their hearts are set upon the pilgrimage. . . . I had rather one day in your courts than a thousand elsewhere; I had rather lie at the threshold of the house of my God then dwell in the tents of wickedness" (83:5-6,11).

[4]Albert Gelin, "La prière du pèlerin au Temple, Ps. 84 (83)," *Bible et Vie chrétienne*, XIX (1955), 82-92. Dom Thierry has commented on several of the songs of ascent in *Jérusalem, cité de Dieu* (2nd edition; Bruges: Abbayede Saint Andre, 1954).

The announcement of a pilgrimage in the near future brings its own joy. "I rejoiced because they said to me, 'We will go up to the house of the Lord'" (121:1). On the way, songs of ascent were sung to the sound of flutes (119-135; cf. Is. 30:29).

These brief songs with their marked rhythm are dominated by the thought of the city of Jerusalem,[5] of Mt. Sion,[6] and of the community, "Israel."[7] They particularly implore peace (*shalom*), alluding to the second part of the name Jerusalem.[8] The songs figure in the Roman Breviary, at Vespers, the first days of the week. Ardor is redoubled as the capital is neared (83:8). Already the divine blessing in the form of an early rain anticipates the wishes of the pilgrims (83:7; cf. Za. 14:16-17).

At last, the wonderful city is reached, the gathering place of Israel, the center of unity:

> And now we have set foot
>   within your gates, O Jerusalem—
> Jerusalem, built as a city
>   with compact unity. (121:2-3)

The new arrivals do not act like gawking tourists, but like fervent believers. Tragic and glorious memories burst forth from the depths of their memories. Jerusalem—reality itself with ramparts, towers, and palaces—has, as other beings, a soul: "Go about Sion,

[5]Pss. 121:2-6; 124:2; 126:1; 127:5.
[6]Pss. 124:1; 125:1; 127:5; 128:5; 131:13; 132:3; 133:3.
[7]Pss. 120:4; 124:5; 127:6; 128:1; 129:7-8; 130:3.
[8]Pss. 121:6-8; 124:5; 127:6; cf. 119:6-7.

make the rounds; count her towers. Consider her
ramparts, examine her castles, that you may tell a
future generation that such is God, our God forever
and ever" (47:13-15); "Come! behold the deeds of
the Lord" (45:9). As the procession moves on, the
visitors look around and wonder. New life is given to
their memories: "As we had heard, so have we seen
in the city of the Lord of hosts, in the city of our
God . . . O God, we ponder your kindness within
your temple" (47:9-10). "There he shattered the
flashing shafts of the bow, shield and sword, and
weapons of war" (75:4; cf. 45:10; 47:5-8). Among
other astounding feats of the Lord was the famous
defeat of Sennarcherib (701 B.C.). It is called to mind
so that one could look to the future with a calm mind.
One day, the city would be expanded to receive
Egyptians, Ethiopians, Philistines, Tyrians, and Bab-
ylonians. The ancient enemies of Israel would become
citizens of Sion. Those "reborn" would sing and dance,
and proclaim their devotion to the spiritual fatherland:
"My home is with you" (86:7).[9]

God himself keeps the census register up-to-date:
"They shall note, when the peoples are enrolled: 'This
man was born there'" (86:6). To be sure, the mystery
of the Church, the body and spouse of Christ, is not
fully revealed until the New Testament. The mystique
of Sion, however, sketches its main outlines. In his
prayer, the Christian identified Jerusalem with the

[9]Cf. Is. 2:2-4; Mi. 4:1-2; Is. 54; 60; 62.

Church. Dear to God, the mother of the peoples, the Church was an outward sign of unity, a place of the divine presence, a sure refuge for the faithful and harbor of peace, the very antithesis of Babylon (136). The Church prefigured the here below of the assembly of heavens, *Coelestis urbs Jerusalem, beata pacis visio.*

CENTER OF WORSHIP

In Sion, the pilgrims see the God of gods (83:8), his power and his glory (62:4). That is to say, they experienced the good that flows from his presence. They were filled with the good things of his house, the holy things of his temple (64:5). The Lord is committed in favor of Sion:

> I will bless her with abundant provision,
>   her poor I will fill with bread.
> Her priests I will clothe with salvation,
>   and her faithful ones shall shout merrily for joy.
> (131:15-16)

Priests, spokesmen for the Master of the House in the course of the sacred ceremonies,[10] proclaimed in the liturgies of entrance[11] the conditions for obtaining the blessing (23:5; 132:3). These may be summed up in a single word: purity—purity of hands, of clothing, and of heart (23:4-6; cf. the "decalogue" of Psalm 14). At times, the importance given ritual acts by the psalmists is astonishing. In reality, the Psalter, as a whole, contains a well-balanced doctrine. Without

---

[10]Cf. 11, 20, 59, 80, 94, 109.
[11]Pss. 14; 23; cf. Mi. 6:6-8; Is. 33:14-16.

dispositions of heart, exterior demonstrations were reduced to empty and hypocritical gestures. If they were joined with wicked feelings, they were displeasing to God.

> Why do you recite my statutes,
>   and profess my covenant with your mouth,
>   though you hate discipline
>   and cast my words behind you?
> When you see a thief coming you keep pace with him,
>   and with adulterers you throw in your lot.
> To your mouth you give free rein for evil,
>   you harness your tongue to deceit.
> You sit speaking against your brother;
>   against your mother's son you spread rumor.
> When you do these things, shall I be deaf to it?
> Or think you that I am like yourself?
> I will correct you by drawing them up before your eyes.
> (49:16-21)

The terror of these vengeful words continues to disquiet consciences. The same psalmist determines the exact importance of the liturgical offerings. In itself, the multiplication of sacrifices does not honor God, for the Lord is not a debtor to man, but man is God's client:

> Not for your sacrifices do I rebuke you,
>   for your holocausts are before me always.
> I take from your house no bullock,
>   no goats out of your fold.
> For mine are all the animals of the forest,
>   beasts by the thousand on my mountains.
> I know all the birds of the air,
>   and whatever stirs in the plains, belongs to me.

If I were hungry, I should not tell you,
  for mine are the world and its fullness.
Do I eat the flesh of strong bulls,
  or is the blood of goats my drink? (49:8-13)[12]

The prophets vigorously insisted, according to the genius of their language, on the primacy of inner religion (Am. 5:24; Os. 6:6; Mi. 6:8). It took Israel a long time to become imbued with this teaching. The enlightening and purifying intervention of God was necessary. It was the Lord who opened the ears of his people (39:7b) to the wisdom that lies in the secret of the heart (50:8). He imposed an austere apprenticeship—separation from the altar of holocausts —during the Exile. Texts on spiritual sacrifice are read in the Psalms relating to the Captivity. This connection is an evocative one:

Sacrifice or oblation you wished not,
  but ears open to obedience you gave me.
Holocausts or sin-offerings you sought not;
  then said I, "behold I come . . .
  to do your will, O my God, is my delight,
  and your law is within my heart!" (39:7-9)

I will praise the name of God in song,
  and I will glorify him with thanksgiving;
  this will please the Lord more than oxen
  or bullocks with horns and divided hoofs.
(68:31-32; cf. 49:14,23)

For you are not pleased with sacrifices;
  should I offer a holocaust, you would not accept it.

12Cf. Is. 1:11 ff.; Jer. 7:21 ff.; Am. 5:21 ff.

My sacrifice, O God, is a contrite spirit;
   a heart contrite and humbled, O God, you will not
   spurn. (50:18-19)

Thus, the divine pedagogue leads men, little by
little, along the path to perfect sacrifice. The cross
will ally the maximum of spirituality with the maximum of giving and the maximum of efficacy.

During their sojourn at Jerusalem, the pilgrims
fulfilled their promises and their vows (64:2). They
shared in the liturgies of the time (64; 66; 106) and,
in particular, in the ceremonies which, on the occasion of the great solemnities (Passover, Pentecost, and
Tabernacles), commemorated the events of sacred history—the departure from Egypt, the gift of the law
on Sinai, the sojourn in the desert. We would like
to know which Psalms were designated for these traditional feasts. But, our information concerns only late
usage. On the evidence of its heading, Psalm 29 was
sung "for the dedication of the House of God." The
Talmud tells us that the little, or Egyptian, *Hallel*
(112-117) was sung during the sacrifice of the lambs
at Passover. Psalm 28 was used during the closing
days of the feast of Tabernacles, as its title in the
Septuagint tells us. While the *Talmud* gives us the
same information for Psalms 49, 64, 80, and 93, Psalms
28 and 67 are assigned to Pentecost.

FORTRESS OF ORTHODOXY

The Teaching of Sacred History: Historical Psalms.
In reality, at all of the annual meetings, the mysteries

of salvation might be recalled, and the Covenant renewed (cf. Pss. 49, 80, 94, 98). It is not only a question of mulling over remembrances, but of reliving them, by bringing them into the present in worship. Some Psalms, similar to a meditated, prayed, and sung catechism, orchestrate the principal themes of history: The patriarchial tradition dominated by the Promise and the Covenant (104); the Exodus, preceded and accompanied by wonders; the journey in the desert, and the revelation of Sinai; and at last, the entrance into the inheritance (77, 104, 105).

The psalmists do not merely number the bare facts; they sift out their religious meaning. They give us "the glories of the Lord" in his glorious deeds (77:4, 32; 104:1,5), testimonies of God's faithfulness (104:8), of his love (77:68), and of his everlasting mercy (135). This glance backwards nourishes praise, thanksgiving, and penance (104; 105). It gives direction to practical attitudes (77:1-8; 104:45).

In the past, grace alternated with sin (77:105). The high deeds of God were in contrast to the misdeeds of a wayward and rebellious people who kept neither a steadfast heart nor a faithful spirit (77:8). "Their hearts were not steadfast toward him, nor were they faithful to his covenant. The Lord, being merciful, forgave their sin and destroyed them not; often he turned back his anger and let none of his wrath be roused. He remembered that they were flesh, a passing breath that returns not" (77:37-39; cf. Dt. 32; Neh. 9).

These instructions of the catechetical past, easy to identify in the Roman Breviary (Matins of Friday and Saturday) make use of a spiritual adventure with a universal bearing (1 Cor. 10:5-11). Each one will discover there the pattern of his own history, as in a delicate tracery. There is overflowing of divine favors, the frequently renewed and disconcerting lack of gratitude, forgetfulness, murmurs, trials of God, offenses, and only superficial conversions. The Jewish people had no monopoly on wasted graces. Happily for us, the mercy of God endures forever.

Benefits and Riches of the Law: Legal Psalms. The historical Psalms emanated from Jerusalem's circle of men of letters—priests, Levites, and wise men. To educate and edify, these official instructors composed and hewed out pieces of various sorts. These are characterized by a style like that of Proverbs, full of schoolmaster preaching, that is, moralizing preoccupation. The alphabetic poems, the acrostics in particular, are attributed to these teachers. Each verse (24, 33, 144), each hemistich (110:111), or each strophe (9, 36, 118) begins with its own consonant that follows the order of the alphabet.

The author of Psalm 118 composed a veritable *tour de force.* He separated 176 verses into 22 strophes, each one devoted to a letter of the alphabet. Furthermore, the eight verses of each strophe begin with the same letter and also contain one of the eight synonyms that designates the Law. These procedures, however helpful to memory, are dangerous to poetry. Even so, they still cannot quite stifle the sincerity and profound piety of the psalmists. Those masters were not primarily concerned with constructing a complicated thesis. They wanted to win love for their teaching by insisting on the happiness that accrued to faithful disciples. This is the reason for their frequent exclamations: "Happy the man . . . who meditates on the Lord day and night" (1:1-2); "Happy is he whose fault is taken away, whose sin is covered" (31:1); "Happy the man who makes the Lord his trust; who turns not to idolatry or to those who stray after falsehood" (39:5); "Happy is he who has regard for the lonely and poor" (40:2; "Happy the man who fears the Lord, who greatly delights in his commands" (111:1); "Happy are they whose way is blameless, who walk in the law of the Lord" (118:1). Here is a gallery of portraits of the happy people:

The man assiduous at meditating on the Law:
He is like a tree, planted near running water,
    that yields its fruit in due season,
    and whose leaves never fade.
(Whatever he does, prospers.) (1:3)

He who fears the Lord:
His posterity shall be mighty upon the earth;
    the upright generation shall be blessed.
Wealth and riches shall be in his house . . .
    he shall never be moved;
    the just man shall be in everlasting remembrance.
An evil report he shall not fear. (111:2-3, 6-7)

For you shall eat the fruit of your handiwork;
  happy shall you be, and favored.
Your wife shall be like a fruitful vine
  in the recesses of your home;
  your children like olive plants around your table.
Behold, thus is the man blessed
  who fears the Lord. (127:2-4)[13]

The man trusting in Providence:
Behold, sons are a gift from the Lord;
  the fruit of the womb is a reward.
Like arrows in the hand of a warrior
  are the sons of one's youth.
Happy the man whose quiver is filled with them . . . .
(126:3-4)

The just man:
The just man shall flourish like the palm tree,
  like a cedar of Lebanon shall he grow.
They that are planted in the house of the Lord
  Shall flourish in the courts of our God.
They shall bear fruit even in old age;
  vigorous and sturdy shall they be. (91:13-15)

The finale of Psalm 127 envisons, beyond an individual or family horizon, the happiness of Jerusalem:
"May you see the prosperity of Jerusalem all the days
of your life!" (127:5.) A royal prayer of thanksgiving,
adapted to the liturgy after the Exile, describes this
prosperity in idyllic accents:

[13]Cf. Evode Beaucamp, "Le secret d'une vie féconde (Ps.
128/127)," *Bible et Vie chrétienne*, XXXV (1960), 35-45;
L. Jacquet, "Le bonheur du juste," *ibid.*, XXXVIII (1960),
35-42.

May our sons be like plants
   well-nurtured in their youth,
   our daughters like wrought columns
   such as stand at corners of the temple.
May our garners be full,
   affording every kind of store;
   may our sheep be in the thousands,
   and increase to myriads in our meadows;
   May our oxen be well laden.
May there be no breach in the walls,
   no exile,
   no outcry in our streets.
Happy the people for whom things are thus;
   happy the people whose God is the Lord. (143:12-15)

These are the benefits the pilgrims to Jerusalem hoped for by their vows—for themselves, their families, and their nation. To be sure, the Christian is not forbidden to desire temporal goods nor to hope for them, but he ranks earthly food below heavenly happiness. The psalmists enjoyed their happiness only in the land of the living. This concept presupposes a network of notions about the physical constitution of man, and his condition in the world beyond, also about the imperfectly known modalities of God's justice. Today we have more insights.

Following the example of the wise men of Israel, Jesus drew his disciples by the promise of the beatitudes (Mt. 5:3 ff.). But these beatitudes produced a resonance hitherto unheard. Today, as in the past, happiness depends essentially on obedience to the will of God, to his Word. The Christian, freed from the Mosaic law, is "not without the law of God, but under the law of Christ" (1 Cor. 9:21). The praises of the Law (1; 18:8 ff.; 118) are transformed into praises of the Gospel:

> The Law of the Lord is perfect,
>   refreshing the soul;
>   the decree of the Lord is trustworthy,
>   giving wisdom to the simple.
> The precepts of the Lord are right,
>   rejoicing the heart;
> The command of the Lord is clear,
>   enlightening the eye;
> The fear of the Lord is pure,
>   enduring forever;
> The ordinances of the Lord are true,
>   all of them just;
> They are more precious than gold,
>   than a heap of purest gold;
> Sweeter also than syrup
>   or honey from the comb. (18:8-11)

Psalm 118, which runs through all the little hours of Sunday, by the regularity of its monotonous pattern invites us to concentrate on the attachment, the faithfulness, the love that the poet vowed to the Law of Christ. Wisdom, truth, and the life of prudence and knowledge, light and joy, consolation and comfort, deliverance, peace and life, are all benefits that come to us today from the Word of God Incarnate.[14]

---

[14]Cf. Evode Beaucamp, "La gloire de Dieu et la Loi, Ps. 19 (18)," *Bible et Vie chrétienne*, XLIII (1962), 27-41; Hilaire Duesberg, "Le miroir du fidèle, Ps. 119 (118)," *ibid.*, XV (1956), 87-97.

Initiation to Wisdom: The "Philosophical" Psalms.
Some poems do not seem destined for worship. In
these, the wise men sounded hidden depths of history
(77:2) and searched for the meanings of the Law.
These touched on some thorny questions, in particular,
on the problem of reward and punishment. Facts do
not always fit the traditional beliefs, for the wicked
do succeed and the just fail. This is an agonizing
anomaly for believers.[15]

There are voices raised in order to forestall that
scandal. Such is the voice of that imperturbable old
man, who, strong with the strength of faith and experience, remains obstinate in his optimism. To be
sure, everything is going very well for evildoers who
are living happily while the just are suffering. This
may be so, but be patient: "Neither in my youth, nor
now that I am old, have I seen a just man forsaken
nor his descendants begging bread. Though he fall,
he does not lie prostrate, for the hand of the Lord
sustains him. I saw a wicked man, fierce, and stalwart
as a flourishing, age-old tree. And as I passed by, lo!
he was no more; I sought him, but he could not be
found" (36:24-25, 35-36).

Another acrostic poem inculcates the identical lesson
that a virtuous life is a happy life. "Many are the
troubles of the just man, but out of them all the Lord
delivers him; he watches over all his bones; not one
of them is broken. Vice slays the wicked" (33:20-22).

[15]Jer. 12:1-5; 31:29; Jb. 21:7-15; Sir. 8:14; Hab. 1.

Unfortunately, cruel reality often runs counter to these principles. Other psalmists, then, utter almost despairing cries (12:2-4; 38), undergo a veritable crisis of faith (72). Still others, honed by trial, sharpen their ideals and their sentiments as well (118). Some, it seems, have a presentiment of a retribution that will re-establish the balance in the afterlife that no longer exists in the here below.[16] One of them cries out: "But God will redeem me from the power of the nether world by receiving me" (48:16). It may be that he envisaged a division between sinners and righteous in the world beyond the grave (48:15-16). Another, badly shaken, recovers his equanimity after having been close enough to brush against a fall, yet not fall (72:1-17). As for the prosperity of the wicked, it is no more than an illusion, a dream, and a snare. As for the destiny of the just man secure in his faithfulness, it is described:

> Yet with you I shall always be;
>> you have hold of my right hand;
> With your counsel you guide me,
>> and in the end you will receive me in glory.
> Whom else have I in heaven?
> And when I am with you, the earth delights me not.
> Though my flesh and my heart waste away,
>> God is the rock of my heart and my portion forever.
> (72:23-26)

[16]Jacques Guillet, "L'entrée du juste dans la gloire, Ps. 73 (72)," *Bible et Vie chrétienne*, IX (1955), 58-70; A. Rose, "Le sort du riche et du pauvre," *ibid.*, XXXVII (1961), 53-61.

In his uneasiness of mind and heart, comparable to the mystic experience of the saints, this psalmist, a Levite imbued with wisdom and piety, has an intuition of a truth that God will cause to be discovered by his people in the midst of trial.[17] Light comes through the cross. Progress in light is tied to the hard apprenticeship of suffering. This fruitful thought is gathered from a study of the Psalter. Indeed, there can be no doubt that the sorrows of the Exile and the spiritual retreat of the Captivity purified the ideals and the hopes of Israel. Far from Jerusalem, the exiles dreamed of an ideal Sion. When the kingship was no more, they turned toward the King of the future, a monarch according to God's own heart. In their contact with other nations, they reflected on the role of non-Jews in the future kingdom of God. This weakened their traditional particularism.

The men of letters who worked to spread the light of the sanctuary gave the Psalter its final character. They collected and organized the liturgical patrimony, after having retouched some of the Psalms. They added some compositions to the poems of worship that came from their own schools of wisdom. Thanks to them, the hymn book of the Temple also became a book of meditation and edification. To them also is probably owed the present preface of the Psalter (1 and 2). This prelude, especially, sets in relief two

[17]Wis. 3:1-9; Dn. 12:2-3; 2 Mc. 7; 12:44-46.

aspects of the overall collection: (1) its value as teaching, and (2) its Messianic character.

THE SUPREME JOY

In Jerusalem, as the pilgrims prayed, entered into meetings, and edified one another, they also welded together the links of brotherhood. A very short Psalm boasts of that communion between hearts and souls. This is sweet and smooth, like exquisite perfume. Like the oil of priestly consecrations, it is spread in profusion over the head, runs down on the beard, and spills over onto the collar of the cloak. It does good, like the dew descending from Hermon in such abundance that it reaches the hills of Sion (132:2-3). This is an unforgettable experience.

> If I forget you, Jerusalem,
>   may my right hand be forgotten!
> May my tongue cleave to my palate
>   if I remember you not,
>   if I place not Jerusalem
>   ahead of my joy. (136:5-6)

[9]

The Great King

An unhappy man of faith, the community in trial, one whose prayer has been heard, the king, Jerusalem —these are the principal centers of interest in the supplications, thanksgivings, royal poems, and songs of Sion. Nonetheless, the praise of God permeates all of these songs. The permanent presence of this element of praise justifies the Hebrew title of the Psalter: The Book of Praises. In truth, every prayer renders homage to God. The sick proclaim the Lord as their health, the innocent as their refuge, the oppressed as their avenger and their liberator. Sinners recognize him as the unfailing source of pardon. The king turns toward God, his father and his faithful support. Finally, the glory of Jerusalem reflects that of the Dweller in Sion. These suppliants praise God to gain his good will and to give foundation to their assurance. They thank him in advance, as a benefactor who never hides himself from one who prays confidently. As for thanksgiving, it normally includes a eulogy on the divine goodness. There are exegetes who speak at times of the contamination of types. In reality, an attitude of soul as complex as that of man at prayer is never evident in simplified, uniform, and homogeneous forms. The throbbing of his heart bursts all frameworks. The Psalter, however, does include a group of prayers that concentrate on the glorification of God. These are the hymns.[1]

THE HYMNS: THEIR STRUCTURE

This literary family is distinguished by certain characteristic traits. One of these is an invitatory, more or less extended. Sometimes it is an exclamation (8:2; cf. 83:2; 141:1), or a proclamation (92:1; 96:1; 98:1), that gives the signal for the alleluia in the first verses. The psalmist manifests his joy and his enthusiasm in these. No one is dragged to liturgical service; he runs there with haste, drawing with him a crowd of adorers.[2] That is why the invitatory— equivalent to the invocation of prayers of pleading— builds up verbs with varying moods to express the intensity of feeling: praise . . . exalt . . . glorify . . . bless . . . cry out for the Lord . . . sing . . . publish . . . play music . . . clap hands . . . utter cries of joy . . . let praise resound in the assembly . . . let us sing . . . and let us rejoice . . . let the sons of Sion exalt . . . let the drum and harp be played . . . bless, oh my soul . . . praise, oh my soul . . . I want to

[1]Pss. 8; 18:1-7; 28, 32, 46, 64, 65, 66, 67, 74, 75; 80: 1-6; 91, 92, 94:1-7; 95, 96, 97, 98, 99, 102, 103, 110, 112, 113, 116, 133, 134, 135, 144, 145, 146, 147, 148, 149, 150.

[2]Hilaire Duesberg, "Le Psaume invitatoire, Ps. 95 (94)," *Bible et Vie chrétienne*, XII (1955-1956), 83-90.

praise . . . I want to celebrate . . . I want to bless the Lord at all times.

The choir leader sends forth his call to all creatures, to the community, servants of the Lord,[3] descendants of Abraham, sons of Jacob, chosen of God (104:6), and sons of Sion (149:2). He appeals to diverse classes of people, to the house of Israel, house of Aaron, house of Levi (117:2-3; cf. 113:18-20); nations of the earth, islands,[4] and to the elements of nature—heaven, earth, and sea[5]—even worshipers in the heavenly worship, the sons of God (28:2). All of the singers gather around the psalmists for a catholic and cosmic praise. Even in individual recitation, we should consider ourselves the mouthpiece of the universe, the echo of unnumbered voices in the world.

> Come, let us sing joyfully to the Lord;
>> let us acclaim the Rock of our salvation.
> Let us greet him with thanksgiving;
>> let us joyfully sing psalms to him . . .
> Come, let us bow down in worship;
>> let us kneel before the Lord who made us. (94:1-2,6)

The prelude sets the tone and creates an atmosphere of joy. It also reveals to us the environment in which these songs were born. Some invitatories expressly mention the sanctuary—its gates and its courts,[6] its liturgical ornaments (28:2; cf. 95:9), the assembly, ritual

---

[3]Pss. 32:1; 46:1; 112:1; 134:1.
[4]Pss. 65:1; 95:1; 96:1; 99:1.
[5]Ps. 148; cf. Gn. 1; Dn. 3:52-90.
[6]Pss. 99:4; 133:1-2; 150:1.

gestures and attitudes, prostrations, kneelings, and dances.[7] Psalm 150 enumerates the instruments of the sacred orchestra, "the musical instruments of God" (1 Par. 16:42)—trumpet, lyre, harp, timbrel, strings, pipe, and cymbals.[8] The hymns, then, were composed to be chanted or declaimed, to be played with rhythm, sometimes even to be mimed, but always in a climate of spiritual well-being, at the time of Israel's feasts. In private prayer, our hearts at least should sing and our bodies be joined as much as possible to the movements of the soul.

At times in the opening of the Psalm, the poet suggests reasons for praise (135:1; 146:1). He unfolds and spreads them out in the central part, the body of the poem, corresponding to the presentation of the case in supplications and thanksgivings. The attributes of God and his lofty deeds in history and creation are recalled.

The Leader of Israel

In the beginning, Israel celebrated the mighty deeds of God in her favor (Ex. 15:21; Jgs. 5). Israel's praise was not supported by metaphysical considerations but sprang from real experience. The psalmists' ovation exalts God as a hero, head of the tribes, leader of armies, enthroned on the Ark, surrounded with glory, and acclaimed to the sound of the trumpet. The Lord of Israel possesses, and indeed exercises, royal preroga-

---

[7]Pss. 94:6; 95:9; 99:2-4; 110:1; 133:1-2; 150:1, 4.
[8]Cf. 32:2; 80:3; 97:5; 146:7; 149:3.

tives. He ruled the people of the Covenant before reigning over the Holy Land in the sanctuary that lies in its capital. Still, at the beginning, the Hebrews rarely gave him the explicit title of king.[9] The reason for this reserve is doubtful. It may have been faithfulness to a tradition that did not know this appellation. Or, it may have been distrust of a qualification, contaminated by the doubtful character of earthly royalty. God was venerated under the name of *Yahweh*, the Actual, always present and always active, continually helping and protecting his people. This sacred name predominates in the Psalter beside the generic term *Elohim*, God (in the Elohist Psalms). Two ancient names also are found: *Shaddai*, "the god of the mountain" (67:15; 90:1), and *Yahweh* of Armies.[10] One of the oldest fragments, preserved in Psalm 23, identifies, doubtless for the first time, Yahweh of Armies and the King of glory: "Who is this king of glory?—the Lord (Yahweh) strong and mighty, the Lord, mighty in battle, the Lord of hosts" (23:8-10). The Lord appeared with this aura of the warrior king in an equally archaic passage in a processional Psalm:

O God when you went forth at the head of your people,
    when you marched through the wilderness,
        the earth quaked; it rained from heaven at the presence of God,

[9]Nm. 23:21; 24:7, 8; Ex. 15:18; Dt. 33:5; cf. Is. 6; Mi. 4:7; So. 3:15.
[10]Pss. 23:10; 45:8, 12; 47:9; 58:6; 68:7; 79:5, 8, 15, 20; 32:2, 4, 9, 13; 88:9.

at the presence of God, the god of Israel. [This is
  Sinai.] (67:8-9)
They view your progress, O God,
  the progress of my God, my King, into the sanctuary.
(67:25; cf. Jgs. 5:4-5; Dt. 32:2 ff.)

It is again the leader of armies who is glorified in
the primitive substratum of a more austere poem. He
is destined to commemorate and to insure the enthronement of Yahweh on Mount Sion. The Lord conquers
the territory for the benefit of his people. He brings
the peoples into subjection, makes vassals of their
princes, drives out the local divinity, and takes the
name of the Most High, the sublime (Gn. 14:18),
as his own. He becomes the great King over all the
earth (46:3). Fallen are all the false Gods, accomplices
of injustice and disorder. The Lord alone remains as
master of the nations and judge of the earth (81).

THE LORD OF CREATION: THE COSMIC HYMNS

The mighty work of creation which takes preced-
ence for us—*I believe in one God, the creator*—does
not have this privileged place in primitive hymnology,
although it is assumed everywhere that the God who
governed Israel created the world and keeps it in
being.[11] A number of texts celebrate the exploit of
the Creator as a royal victory. It is important to understand these passages correctly, viewing them from
the ideology of the ancient Near East.

---

[11]Cf. G. Lambert, "La Création dans la Bible," *Nouvelle
Revue Théologique*, LXXV (1953), 252-81.

Marduk and Baal had won their princely pre-eminence with a great struggle that ended in victory over the powers of primitive chaos. The Hebrews, on their arrival in Canaan, wondered at the spectacle of the waves which beat against the coasts of Palestine without ever passing beyond the shore. It was their God, the one God, who had mastered this unstable and fearsome sea where mysterious monsters lived. The immigrants had already possessed faith and belief in God, ruler of the world (Gn. 2). Subsequently, they illustrated this truth with images borrowed from Canaanite folklore, under the inspiration of their new experience.[12]

> The Lord is king, in splendor robed;
> > robed is the Lord and girt about with strength;
> > and he has made the world firm,
> > not to be moved.
> Your throne stands firm from of old;
> > from everlasting you are, O Lord.
> The floods lift up, O Lord,
> > the floods lift up their voice;
> > the floods lift up their tumult.
> More powerful than the roar of many waters,
> > more powerful than the breakers of the sea—
> > powerful on high is the Lord. (92:1-4)

God, robed in royal magnificence and girded with the power of a warrior, masters the tumultuous waves of the ocean, gives stability to the world, and sets his throne in the heavens where he defies his enemies,

[12]L. Lègrand, "La création, triomphe cosmique de Yahvé," *Nouvelle Revue Théologique*, LXXXIII (1961), 449-70.

the adversary, and the rebel (8:2). More precise reminiscences depict the primordial combat with a sobriety that separates them from the pagan legends. The myth becomes poetry:

> You stirred up the sea by your might;
>> you smashed the heads of the dragons in the waters.
> You crushed the heads of Leviathan,
>> and made food of him for the dolphins. (73:13-14)
> You rule over the surging of the sea;
>> you still the swelling of its waves.
> You have crushed Rahab with a mortal blow;
>> with your strong arm you have scattered your enemies. (88:10-11)
> . . . Above the mountains the waters stood
>> at your rebuke they fled,
>> at the sound of your thunder they took to flight;
> As the mountains rose, they went down the valleys
>> to the place you had fixed for them.
> You set a limit they may not pass,
>> nor shall they cover the earth again. (103:7-9)

Victorious, God sits as king above the higher ocean in the midst of the "sons of God" who proclaim his glory and his power:

> The Lord is enthroned above the flood;
>> the Lord is enthroned as king forever. (28:10)
> Give to the Lord, you sons of God,
>> give to the Lord glory and praise,
>> give to the Lord the glory due his name;
>> adore the Lord in holy attire. (28:1-2)

From his heavenly throne, the royal king sends forth the powerful, striking, and fearful voice of his thunder.

Christian hymnology also applies to God the epithet of the high Thunderer (Lauds of Friday).

> The voice of the Lord is over the waters,
>   the God of glory thunders,
>   the Lord, over vast waters.
> The voice of the Lord is mighty;
>   The voice of the Lord is majestic.
> The voice of the Lord breaks the cedars,
>   The Lord breaks the cedars of Lebanon.
> He makes Lebanon leap like a calf
>   and Sarion like a young wild bull.
> The voice of the Lord strikes fiery flames;
>   the voice of the Lord shakes the desert,
>   the Lord shakes the wilderness of Cades.
> The voice of the Lord twists the oaks and strips the forests,
>   and in his temple all say, "Glory!" (28:3-9)

Israel did not represent God with painted or sculptured figures. To make up for this, Israel was happy to recall the perfections of the Creator's work by drawing on a stock of images, furnished by its ethnic culture and psychology. Through this poetic artifice, the Lord appears truly living and active. In the hymns, the descriptions of nature reveal not only a poetic vision of the cosmos, they especially imply a religious contemplation. The phenomena of the weather and the alternation of the seasons hide, and yet reveal, divine intervention. Transfigured nature signifies God and lets the tracery of his presence shine through. Here are some provocative examples:

You water the mountains from your palace;
　the earth is replete with the fruit of your works.
You raise grass for the cattle.
　and vegetation for men's use,
　producing bread from the earth,
　and wine to gladden men's hearts,
　so that their faces gleam with oil,
　and bread fortifies the hearts of men. (103:13-15)
You have visited the land and watered it;
　greatly have you enriched it.
God's water courses are filled;
　you have prepared the grain.
Thus have you prepared the land: drenching its furrows,
　breaking up its clods,
　softening it with showers,
　blessing its yield.
You have crowned the year with your bounty,
　and your paths overflow with the rich harvest;
The untilled meadows overflow with it,
　and rejoicing clothes the hills,
　the fields are garmented with flocks
　and the valleys blanketed with grain . . . (64:10-14)

This extraordinarily fresh description uses poetic terms to comment on the theological affirmation of Psalm 66: "The earth has yielded its fruits; God, our God, has blessed us" (v. 7). The privileged beneficiary of these gifts is man, "a little less than the angels and crowned with honor and glory," master of creation (8:4-9). But the divine condescension is extended to *all* beings, right down to the young ravens who cry out for their food (146:9). It is enough to read the

magnificent developments of Psalm 103 to be convinced
of this.

Some exegetes connect certain passages of the cosmic
hymns with extrabiblical literature. The song of the
storm (28) recalls the praises in honor of the Phoe-
nician Baal. It may be that the beginning of Psalm
18 contains a reference to the prayers of Shamash,
sun god of the Assyro-Babylonians. The canticle of
creation (103) is probably inspired by the great hymn
to Aton. But the psalmists were not making pastiches,
they were dispossessing their rivals of Ras Shamrah of
Babylon and Egypt. They always sang of the one God.
If they borrowed, they assimilated what they borrowed.
Their alchemy transmutes everything. There is no trace
of nature worship in their work, for God is not confounded with the power of the cosmos. "He who rides
on the heights of the ancient heavens" (67:34) masters the world by his transcendence.

Besides, faithful to her own genius, Israel was not
inclined to mythological fantasies, but placed historical
allusions over cosmic themes. These strands are at
times so closely interwoven that we can hardly untangle
them. Psalm 73 (13-15) recalls the work of creation
and brings back in tracery the passage of the Red Sea,
the miracles of the desert, and the crossing of the
Jordan. The monsters of the deep (Rahab, Leviathan)
symbolize the adversaries of the Jewish people. Many
exegetes explain the fragment (vv. 10-11) of Psalm

88 in the same way. In Psalm 28, the desert of Cades brings Sinai to mind. The divine throne, raised from all eternity on the heights of heaven (92:2), turns the mind to the Temple of Jerusalem, where holiness lasts for length of days (92:5). To the unchangeable laws of nature (92:1) correspond the "witnesses" of revelation (92:5). The glory of God is sung by the universe (18:2-7) and made even more manifest in the Law (18:8-11).

The greater part of the hymns, composed after the Exile, unfold the same motives of praise. But meanwhile, the themes have matured and have been purified through theological elaboration and the reflection of Wisdom.[13] "By the word of the Lord the heavens were made; by the breath of his mouth all their host. For he spoke, and it was made; he commanded and it stood forth" (32:6,9; cf. Gn. 1). "He commanded and they [the heavens and the stars] were created" (148:5). "All that the Lord wills he does in heaven and on earth, in the seas and all the deeps" (134:6). The psalmists never weary of magnifying this absolute supremacy. They repeat to satiety the attributes of the King of heaven and earth—his power and majesty, justice and faithfulness, goodness and mercy. Transcendence is strongly advocated, sometimes pointedly against the folly of idolatry (113:12-15; 134:15-18).

[13]Pss. 32, 94, 113, 134, 135, 145, 146, 147, 148.

SOVEREIGN OF THE NATIONS: SONGS OF THE KINGDOM

King of Israel, king of creation, the Lord exercises and will exercise his suzerainty over all nations of the earth. This idea, dear to Deutero Isaiah, characterizes a series of hymns (95-98) that re-echo the acclamation: "The Lord is King!"[14]

Good cheer overflows as it does on a day of consecration. Israel, the people, the islands, all the elements of the universe, break into shouts of joy. Psalm 96 describes the coming of the Master of the world as a theophony whose details recall that of Sinai. "Clouds and darkness are round about him, justice and judgment are the foundation of his throne. Fire goes before him and consumes his foes round about. His lightnings illumine the world; the earth sees and trembles. The mountains melt like wax before the Lord, before the Lord of all the earth" (96:2-5). In this triumph, Israel keeps a privileged role,[15] but the kingdom is enlarged to the full dimensions of the universe in a world renewed: "The Lord comes to rule the earth. He shall rule the world with justice and the peoples with his constancy" (95:13). The false gods of other nations are reduced to nothingness. Chastised are the servants and adorers of idols. The divine glory shines everywhere with the good news of salvation (95:2-3). Light dawns for the just, and

[14]Pss. 95:10; 96:1; 98:1.
[15]Pss. 95:10; 96:8; 97:1-3; 98:4-5.

gladness for the upright of heart (96:11). In Christian voices, the songs of the kingdom take on the accent of a missionary prayer.[16]

Reading this group of Psalms (95-98 and 93-94, 99 added as preface and conclusion), one has the impression that the editors of the Psalter assembled the songs used for a liturgical feast, celebrating the universal royalty of the Lord, Creator and Master of history. These hypotheses may be left to the exegetes. For us, these new (95:1; 97:1) songs expressed, with much fervor and happiness, faith in the one God, religious universalism, and the assurance of the "coming" of the Lord. They form a natural epilogue to this summary study of the Psalter. Even in the deepest darkness, the psalmists looked to a happy future because they were supported by God alone, the hope of all the ends of the earth (64:6). Individuals, kings, community, even the earth itself are waiting for "salvation."

CONCLUSION

To be sure, many of the supplications were written in tears and blood. In this Book, praise and thanks-

[16]André Feuillet, "Les psaumes eschatologiques du règne de Yahweh," *Nouvelle Revue Théologique*, LXXIII (1951), 244-60, 352-63; A. Rose, "Le Règne du Dieu-Saint. Lecture juive du Psaume 99 (98)"; "Celui qui siège sur les Chérubins. Lecture chrétienne du Psaume 99 (98)," *Bible et Vie chrétienne*, XIX (1957), 91-99; XX (1957-58), 101-8; A. Strobel, *La conversion des gentils dans les Psaumes* (Paris: Gabalda; and Ottawa: University of Ottawa, 1950).

giving do not succeed in stifling cries of terror, protests against injustice, clamors of war, or outbreaks of vengeance. The Psalms were made of the stuff of mankind itself. There is always a light, flaming or subdued, that gleams in the night. It is the invincible faith in a just and good God who heals broken hearts, binds up man's wounds, frees the oppressed, feeds the hungry, sets free the captives, gives sight to the blind, straightens up the bowed down, supports the orphan and the widow, pardons all faults. And yet, in spite of all our inconstancies, he remains faithful to his promises (102, 145, 146). That is why our Psalter is, and will always continue to be, the Book of Hope.

Bibliography

Since the Bibliography in the French edition is a notable contribution to the subject of the book, it has been retained. The works cited here are, in general, easily available. Technical works that may be of interest to some readers are listed, as well as translations of special interest for use in prayer. The Bibliography is arranged according to the dates of publication. English translations have been given where they are available. The dates of the original versions are given where a translation takes the place of the original on the list.

TEXTS

Latin Translations

Liber Psalmorum cum Canticis Brevarii Romani. Nova ex testibus primigeniis interpretation latin cum notis criticis et exegeticis cura Professorum Pontificii Instituti Biblici, editio secunda. Editio Americana a Pontificio Instituto Approbata. (New York: Benziger Brothers, Inc., 1945).

Psalterii secundum Vulgatam Bibliorum Versionem Nova Recensio iuxta votum Synodi Generalis Abbatum Ordinis Sancti Benedicti cura et studio Roberti Weber monachi Claravallensis edita. (Clervaux, Luxembourg: Abbaye Saint Maurice et Saint Maur, 1961).

English Translations

Ronald Knox, *The Psalms: A New Translation.* New York: Sheed & Ward, 1947. [This mannered translation into prose faces the challenge of translating even Psalm 118 into an alphabetic acrostic.]

The Book of Psalms and the Canticles of the Roman Breviary, by Members of the Catholic Biblical Association of America, Paterson, New Jersey: St. Anthony Guild Press, 1950.

The Psalms: A New Translation. London: Fontana Books, Collins: 1963. [This translation seeks to keep close to the Hebrew original while remaining singable.]

COMMENTARIES

Jean Calès, *Le Livre des Psaumes traduit et commenté.* Paris: Gabriel Beauchesne, 1936. I, II. [Somewhat old, but still useful.]

E. Pannier, *Les Psaumes.* Paris: Letouzey et Ané, 1937. [This solid commentary was completely revised with the addition of the new Latin Psalter and the adaptation of the commentary to it by H. Renard in 1950.]

M. Lepin, *Le Psautier logique. Les psaumes logiquement distribués, traduits et commentés pour le Bréviaire et la piéte.* Paris, Bloud et Gay, 1937. I, II. [Grouping by doctrinal themes, with an index of ideas found in the Psalms.]

Mgr. J. J. Weber, *Le Psautier du Bréviaire Romain.* Paris: Desclée et Compagnie, 1951[5]. [Short but substantial.]

E. Podechard, *Le Psautier. Traduction littérale et explication Historique.* Lyons: Jourjon, 1954. I (Pss. 1-75), (Pss. 76-100, 110). [Unfortunately, this scientific work is incomplete. It also lacks an introduction.]

E. J. Kissane, *The Book of Psalms.* Dublin: Browne and Nolan, 1953, 1955. I, II. [Standard introduction and brief commentary.]

A. Chouraqui, *Les Psaumes traduits et presentés*. Paris: Presses Universitaires de France, 1956. [The author's own translation with a commentary following the Jewish tradition of the Middle Ages.]

E. Dhorme, *La Bible, l'Ancien Testament*. Paris: Gallimard, 1959. II. [A faithful translation with succinct notes.]

Giorgio Castellino, *Libro dei Salmi*. Turin: Marietti, 1959.[2] [A notable work including a study of the literary forms and a judicious use of extrabiblical comparisons.]

Hans-Joachim Kraus, *Psalmen*. Neukirchen: Neukirchen Verlag, 1958-1960. I, II. [One of the better and fuller Protestant commentaries. Two ministers, A. Maillot and A. Lelièvre, have begun the publication of a commentary in which scientific care is linked with apostolic concern: *Les Psaumes*. Geneva: Labor et Fides, 1962. I, Pss. 1-50.]

Special Studies

Jean Steinmann, *Les Psaumes*. Paris: Gabalda, 1951. [Analysis of a number of classes of Psalms placed in their historical setting.]

Albert Gelin, *The Poor of Yahweh*. Trans. Kathryn Sullivan; Collegeville, Minnesota: The Liturgical Press, 1964; French edition, 1953. [Analysis of some Psalms in which the piety of the "poor" is expressed.]

Pius Drijvers, *Les Psaumes, genres littéraires et thèmes doctrinaux*. Paris: Éditions du Cerf, 1958. [Excellent.]

Paul Auvray, "Le Livre des Psaumes," André Robert and André Feuillet, editors, 2nd edition, *Introduction a la Bible*. I, pp. 585-622. [Survey of problems about the Psalter.]

G. Pidoux, *Du Portique a l'Autel, Introduction aux Psaumes*. Veuchâtel: Delachaux et Niestlé, 1959. [Short but stimulating.]

Richesses et deficiences des anciens Psautiers Latins. Collectanea Biblica; Rome: Abbaye Saint Jerome, 1959. XIII.

P. E. Bonnard, *Le Psautier selon Jérémie.* Paris: Éditions du Cerf, 1960. [Study of the influence of the prophet on the psalmists.]

Robert de Langhe, editor, *Le Psautier. Ses origines. Ses problèmes littéraires.* Études presentées aux XIIᵉ Journées Bibliques (August 29-30, 1960); Louvain: Publications Universitaires, 1962. [Rich bibliography; exposition of the present state of research on the Psalter.]

A. Barucq, *L'expression de la louange et de la prière dans la Bible et en Égypte.* Cairo: Institut français d'archéologie orientale, 1962. [This work, while first of all intended for the specialist, contains an exhaustive study on the structure of the Psalms.]

Sigmand Mowinckel, *The Psalms in Israel's Worship.* Trans. David Ap-Thomas. Nashville, Tennessee: Abingdon Press, 1962. I, II. [Thorough presentation of theory which has had great influence on modern exegesis.]

THE PSALMS, CHRISTIAN PRAYER

Pierre de Puniet, *Le Psautier liturgique à la lumière de la tradition chrétienne.* Paris: Desclée de Brouwer et Compagnie, 1935. I, II,

Jean Laloux, *Pour mieux prier les Psaumes.* Librairie Brunet: Arras, 1949.

Jean Danielou, "Les Psaumes dans la liturgie de l'Ascension," *La Maison Dieu,* 21: 40-56, 1950.

Louis Bouyer, "Les Psaumes, prière du peuple de Dieu," *La Bible et l'Evangile.* Paris: Éditions du Cerf, 1958.[2]

————, "Priere avec les Psaumes," *La Vie Spirituelle,* 70:81-94, 1944.

————, "The Psalms in the Liturgy," *The Pascal Mystery.* Chicago: Henry Regnery, 1950.

————, "Les Psaumes dans la prière chretiénne traditionelle," *Bible et Vie chrétienne*, 10:22-35, 1955.

Mgr. Garrone, *Psaumes et prière*. Paris: Casterman, 1952.

Hilaire Duesberg, "Note sur l'utilisation du psautier en Caréme," *La Maison Dieu*, 31:120-31, 1952.

"Les Psaumes, prière de l'assemblée chrétienne," *La Maison Dieu*, 33, 1953.

Joseph Gelineau, "Marie dans la prière chrétienne des Psaumes," *La Maison Dieu*, 38:30-55, 1954.

F. Vandenbroucke, *Les Psaumes et le Christ*. Louvain: Centre Liturgique Abbaye de Mont César, 1955.

A. M. Roguet, "Les Psaumes, prière du peuple chrétien," *Fetes et Saisons*, 1955.

M. F. Moos, *Les Psaumes, prière des chrétiens*. Paris: Éditions Ouvrieres, 1956.

Michael Gasnier, *The Psalms School of Spirituality*. Trans. Aldhelm Dean; Saint Louis: B. Herder Book Company, 1962; French edition, 1957.

Gaston Brillet, *Meditations on the Old Testament*, II, *The Psalms*. Trans. Kathryn Sullivan; New York: Desclee Company, 1960; French edition, 1958.

P. Guichou, *Les Psaumes commentés par la Bible*. Paris: Éditions du Cerf, 1959. I, II, III.

Soeur Jeanne d'Arc, "Prier avec les Psaumes," *La Vie Spirituelle*, 103:66-87, 1960.

Augustin George, *Praying the Psalms*. Trans. Richard X. Redmond; Notre Dame, Indiana: Fides Publishers, 1964; French edition, 1963.

Genevieve Vauthier, *Le Psautier des jeunes*. Bruges: Desclée de Brouwer, 1960.

Romano Guardini, *Psaumes et Fêtes*. Trans. M. Ce; Paris: Éditions du Cerf, 1961. I.

M. Le Bas, *Mon Psautier, ma joie*. Paris: Éditions Saint Paul, 1961.

Albert Gelin, *The Psalms Are Our Prayers*. Trans. Michael J. Bell; Collegeville, Minnesota: The Liturgical Press, 1964; French edition, 1961.

Thomas Worden, *The Psalms are Christian Prayer*. New York: Sheed & Ward, 1961.

J. M. Hum and C. Cneude, *Guide Pastoral de Cantiques et Psaumes*. Paris: Éditions du Cerf, 1962.

O. Rimaud and J. Gelineau, *Le Guide du Psautier de la Bible de Jerusalem*. Paris: Éditions du Cerf, 1962.

Romano Guardini, *Psalmengebetbuch*. Munich: Kösel-Verlag, 1963.